Advances in Sentiment Analysis - Techniques, Applications, and Challenges

Edited by Jinfeng Li

Published in London, United Kingdom

Advances in Sentiment Analysis - Techniques, Applications, and Challenges
http://dx.doi.org/10.5772/intechopen.111293
Edited by Jinfeng Li

Contributors
Jinfeng Li, Yohei Seki, K. Victor Rajan, Media Anugerah Ayu, Abdul Haris Muhendra, Saeed Albarhami Thabit, Konstantinos Kyritsis, Nikolaos Spatiotis, Isidoros Perikos, Michael Paraskevas

First published in London, United Kingdom, 2024 by IntechOpen
IntechOpen is the global imprint of INTECHOPEN LIMITED, registered in England and Wales, registration number: 11086078, 5 Princes Gate Court, London, SW7 2QJ, United Kingdom
Printed in Croatia

British Library Cataloguing-in-Publication Data
A catalogue record for this book is available from the British Library

Additional hard and PDF copies can be obtained from orders@intechopen.com

Advances in Sentiment Analysis - Techniques, Applications, and Challenges
Edited by Jinfeng Li
p. cm.

This title is part of the Artificial Intelligence Book Series, Volume 22
Topic: Machine Learning and Data Mining
Series Editor: Andries Engelbrecht
Topic Editor: Marco Antonio Aceves-Fernández

Print ISBN 978-0-85014-060-6
Online ISBN 978-0-85014-061-3
eBook (PDF) ISBN 978-0-85014-062-0
ISSN 2633-1403

For EU product safety concerns:
IN TECH d.o.o., Prolaz Marije Krucifikse Kozulić 3, 51000 Rijeka, Croatia,
info@intechopen.com or visit our website at intechopen.com.

IntechOpen Book Series

Artificial Intelligence

Volume 22

Aims and Scope of the Series

Artificial Intelligence (AI) is a rapidly developing multidisciplinary research area that aims to solve increasingly complex problems. In today's highly integrated world, AI promises to become a robust and powerful means for obtaining solutions to previously unsolvable problems. This Series is intended for researchers and students alike interested in this fascinating field and its many applications.

Meet the Series Editor

Andries Engelbrecht received the Masters and Ph.D. degrees in Computer Science from the University of Stellenbosch, South Africa, in 1994 and 1999 respectively. He is currently appointed as the Voigt Chair in Data Science in the Department of Industrial Engineering, with a joint appointment as Professor in the Computer Science Division, Stellenbosch University. Prior to his appointment at Stellenbosch University, he has been at the University of Pretoria, Department of Computer Science (1998-2018), where he was appointed as South Africa Research Chair in Artifical Intelligence (2007-2018), the head of the Department of Computer Science (2008-2017), and Director of the Institute for Big Data and Data Science (2017-2018). In addition to a number of research articles, he has written two books, Computational Intelligence: An Introduction and Fundamentals of Computational Swarm Intelligence.

Meet the Volume Editor

Prof. Jinfeng Li is a microwave engineer, a specialist in sentiment analysis for big data, and an authority on liquid crystals-based millimeter-wave technology. Prof. Li was a recipient of the Institution of Engineering and Technology (IET) Award, Arthur Jarvis Prize, Annals of Emerging Technologies in Computing (AETiC) Highly Cited Article Award 2023, and Best Paper Awards at the Institute of Electrical and Electronics Engineers (IEEE) and Institute of Physics (IOP) conferences. He was a Cambridge Trust Scholar, Emerging Technologist with Barclays UK, editorial board member of three Science Citation Index journals, and TPC and Session Chair of five IEEE conferences. He was elected Senior Member of the China Institute of Communications, a Newton Prize reviewer for the UK National Commission for UNESCO, and a grants reviewer for the Health and Social Care Delivery Research fund from the National Institute for Health Research, UK. Prof. Li was elected National-level Young Talent in 2023.

Contents

Preface

Understanding the sentiments and emotions expressed in text data is paramount in an era driven by digital communication and social media. Sentiment analysis refers to the process of identifying and extracting opinions, attitudes, and emotions expressed in text, audio, or video data. The book provides a comprehensive overview of the techniques, applications, and challenges associated with sentiment analysis. It covers a range of topics intended for researchers, academics, and professionals who are interested in understanding state-of-the-art sentiment analysis. The main aim of the book is to provide insights into the latest developments in the field and to help readers understand the challenges and opportunities associated with sentiment analysis. The book is unique in that it covers both theoretical and practical aspects of sentiment analysis, and it provides real-world examples and case studies that demonstrate the application of sentiment analysis in different domains. *Advances in Sentiment Analysis – Techniques, Applications, and Challenges* is a valuable resource for anyone looking to stay updated with the latest developments in this exciting field.

Jinfeng Li
Beijing Institute of Technology,
Beijing, China

Section 1

Introduction

Chapter 1

Introductory Chapter: The 2023 Sentiment Analysis Roadmap

Jinfeng Li

1. Introduction

As the introductory chapter of the book, the 2023 Sentiment Analysis Roadmap serves as a concise yet comprehensive (and engaging) overview of the latest trends, techniques, and applications in the field of sentiment analysis. It establishes the foundation for the subsequent content by presenting a panoramic view of the present status and significance of sentiment analysis in today's society. The chapter commences by defining sentiment analysis and illuminating its diverse applications, encompassing market research, customer service, political analysis, healthcare, etc. It then traces the historical trajectory of sentiment analysis, originating from its association with rule-based lexicon, natural language processing and machine learning. The associated challenges and limitations are identified, including the intricate task of accurately interpreting sarcasm and irony, as well as the potential bias stemming from training data, the trade-off between predicting performance and computational resources (cost) with the constraint of labeled training data scarcity, etc. Given the escalating significance of social media and visual content, multimodal sentiment analysis will assume increasing importance for businesses, researchers, and individuals seeking to comprehend sentiment across diverse media types. This chapter also discusses the importance of data quality and ethical considerations in sentiment analysis, such as protecting user privacy and avoiding harmful stereotypes. Finally, the chapter looks ahead to the future of sentiment analysis, discussing emerging trends of integrating diverse sentiment analysis approaches in various domains and applications. It concludes by emphasizing the importance of continued research and development in this rapidly evolving field.

2. Sentiment analysis and its applications

Branching out from big data (both quantitative and qualitative) analytics, sentiment analysis is a rapidly growing field that has gained significant attention in recent years. It involves the use of rule-based lexicon [1], natural language processing (NLP) [2] and other smart techniques [3] to analyze and understand the emotions, opinions, and attitudes expressed in unstructured text data (including but not limited to social media posts, customer reviews, and other online content), and hence to gauge the overall sentiment or opinion (how people feel) of a particular topic or brand (by assessing the polarity of the text) for informed decision making. Bringing valuable data-driven insights for businesses and organizations, sentiment analysis has numerous applications in various industries, including marketing, customer service, politics, and healthcare [4], among others. For example, in the marketing industry, sentiment analysis can be leveraged to analyze customer feedback and identify areas for improvement. In the financial sector, sentiment analysis can be employed to analyze news articles and social media posts to predict market/stock trends [3]. In the education industry, sentiment analysis can be performed to analyze student feedback and identify areas for improvement. Furthermore, AI-powered sentiment analysis can also be used in healthcare to analyze patient feedback and identify areas for improvement. As the demand for sentiment analysis continues to increase, it is essential to formulate a roadmap that outlines the current state of the field and the future direction it is heading. This book and the introductory chapter are thus designed for researchers, practitioners, and decision-makers who are interested in understanding the current state of sentiment analysis and its potential impact on their respective fields. It covers a wide range of topics, including but not limited to the advancements in NLP techniques, the challenges of sentiment analysis in social media, the ethical considerations of sentiment analysis, and the future directions of the field.

3. Methodologies in sentiment analysis

Depending on targeted prediction performance (accuracy and speed) versus computational cost (connected to data complexity in various projects), sentiment analysis can be undertaken in diverse ways, i.e., rule-based approach (which requires a lexicon and weightings for the wordlist to calculate the overall polarity of the text), machine learning-based approach (which requires training with manually tagged labels in order to learn new dataset by supervised learning), and a mix (hybrid approach). **Figure 1** qualitatively compares these methods.

Arguably, artificial intelligence (AI) has revolutionized the field of sentiment analysis in recent years. With the help of machine learning algorithms, AI has made it possible to analyze vast amounts of data and extract valuable insights from it. In this chapter, we will explore the role of AI in sentiment analysis and how it is changing the way we approach this field. One of the key areas where AI has made significant contributions to sentiment analysis is in natural language processing (NLP) that cleans data (preprocessing), constructs the word cloud (tokenization), and transforms words into numbers (vectorization). NLP is a subfield of AI that focuses on the interaction between computers and human language. With the help of NLP, computers can understand and interpret human language, which is essential for sentiment analysis. NLP algorithms can analyze textual data and identify the sentiment expressed in it. They can also identify the tone, emotion, and intent behind the text. This makes it possible to extract valuable insights from social media posts, customer reviews, and other forms of textual data.

In the past decades, AI has significantly contributed to sentiment analysis, particularly in the field of machine learning. Machine learning algorithms have the capability to learn from data and enhance their performance over time, enabling the development of sentiment analysis models that accurately predict the sentiment conveyed in textual data. These algorithms can analyze extensive datasets and discern patterns within the data, thus facilitating predictions for new data instances. Commonly employed supervised learning algorithms, such as Naive Bayes, Support Vector Machines (SVM), and Random Forests, are trained on labeled datasets where

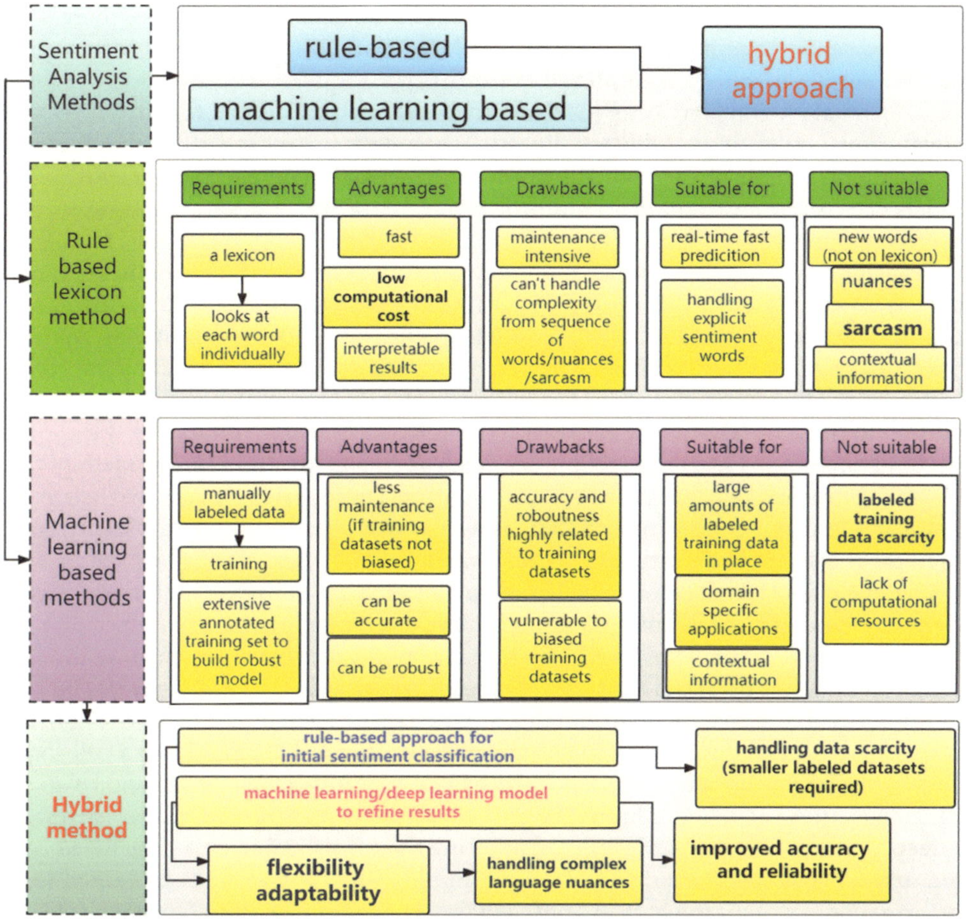

Figure 1.
A qualitative comparison of existing sentiment analysis approaches.

each text is associated with a sentiment label. They acquire knowledge of patterns and relationships between words or features and sentiment labels, enabling the prediction of sentiment for unseen texts.

As sentiment analysis gains popularity, researchers and developers are continually seeking innovative methods to enhance the accuracy and efficiency of sentiment analysis models. Deep learning, a subset of machine learning, focuses on the development of neural networks capable of learning from data. Deep learning algorithms can scrutinize extensive datasets, identifying intricate patterns within the data. Consequently, sentiment analysis models can be developed to accurately predict sentiment expressed in textual data. These algorithms possess the ability to scrutinize text data and identify the sentiments conveyed, as well as perceive the underlying tone, emotion, and intent. Consequently, valuable insights can be extracted from diverse sources of text data, such as social media posts and customer reviews. In recent years, deep learning algorithms, including convolutional neural networks (CNNs) and recurrent neural networks (RNNs), have exhibited great promise in improving sentiment analysis model accuracy. These algorithms excel in learning intricate data patterns and can be trained on extensive datasets to enhance their performance. Recurrent Neural Networks (RNNs) and Long Short-Term Memory (LSTM) networks are often employed to capture the sequential nature of text, while Convolutional Neural Networks (CNNs) effectively extract crucial features through convolutional operations. Additionally, attention mechanisms are utilized to focus on pertinent sections of the text. However, it is essential to note that deep learning models necessitate substantial amounts of labeled data and computational resources for effective training.

Transfer learning has emerged as a noteworthy avenue of exploration in sentiment analysis, involving the utilization of pre-trained models to enhance the performance of sentiment analysis models. This approach enables developers to capitalize on the acquired knowledge derived from training on substantial datasets, thereby improving the accuracy of sentiment analysis models when confronted with smaller datasets. In addition to these notable advancements, researchers are also investigating the application of unsupervised learning techniques, such as clustering and topic modeling, to bolster the precision of sentiment analysis models. These techniques prove instrumental in identifying patterns and themes within text data, subsequently contributing to the refinement of sentiment analysis models.

The integration of the aforementioned methods to capitalize on their respective advantages and mitigate their individual limitations has led to the emergence of a hybrid approach. As depicted in **Figure 1**, it is noteworthy that deep learning models often necessitate substantial amounts of labeled training data, which may not be readily accessible across diverse domains or languages. In such scenarios, the hybrid approach presents notable advantages. Specifically, it involves employing a rule-based component for preliminary sentiment classification [5] utilizing predefined rules or lexicons, thus requiring minimal labeled data. Subsequently, a machine learning or deep learning component is utilized to refine the results using smaller labeled datasets, consequently reducing data requirements while achieving commendable performance. As such, the hybrid approach is anticipated to assume a pivotal role in the future of sentiment analysis. As these techniques continue to evolve and advance, we can anticipate further enhancements in the accuracy and efficiency of sentiment analysis models, rendering them even more invaluable for enterprises and organizations seeking to extract insights from customer feedback and social media data.

4. The rise of multimodal sentiment analysis

As we approach the year 2024, the domain of sentiment analysis is swiftly advancing to encompass not only text-based data but also other modalities. The surge in popularity of social media platforms such as Instagram and TikTok, which heavily rely on visual content, necessitates the development of sentiment analysis tools capable of analyzing both textual and visual elements. Multimodal sentiment analysis represents the frontier of this field, encompassing the analysis of diverse data types, including text, images, videos, and audio. This approach enables a more comprehensive comprehension of sentiment by considering the nuanced characteristics of various media types.

The development of multimodal sentiment analysis tools encounters a significant challenge regarding the availability of extensive labeled datasets. While numerous datasets for text-based sentiment analysis exist, the availability of datasets encompassing images or videos is comparatively limited. Consequently, researchers are striving to construct new datasets that integrate multiple data types, facilitating the training of more accurate and effective multimodal sentiment analysis models. Another challenge lies in the necessity for sophisticated algorithms capable of analyzing and interpreting diverse media types. Analyzing sentiment in an image, for instance, demands distinct skills compared to sentiment analysis in textual content. Consequently, researchers are engaged in the development of novel algorithms that can effectively analyze disparate media types and integrate them within a unified sentiment analysis model.

Notwithstanding these challenges, multimodal sentiment analysis offers substantial potential benefits. By incorporating diverse data types, a more comprehensive understanding of sentiment pertaining to specific content can be achieved. This holds notable value for businesses and organizations reliant on social media platforms to establish connections with their customers, as it enables a better grasp of their brand's perception across various media modalities. As we approach 2023, a surge in research and development efforts in the realm of multimodal sentiment analysis is anticipated.

5. Data quality and ethical considerations in sentiment analysis

The rising popularity and significance of sentiment analysis as a vital tool for businesses and organizations underscore the paramount importance of data quality. The accuracy and dependability of sentiment analysis outcomes are heavily contingent upon the caliber of the data employed for training and testing the models. Data quality encompasses aspects of completeness, consistency, and accuracy pertaining to the data utilized in sentiment analysis. Inaccurate or incomplete data may yield biased or unreliable outcomes, potentially leading to consequential ramifications for businesses and organizations. Ensuring data quality poses a notable challenge due to the sheer volume of unstructured data available on the internet. Social media platforms, blogs, and forums generate an extensive influx of data on a daily basis, rendering it arduous to filter out irrelevant or low-quality information. In response to this challenge, techniques encompassing data cleaning and preprocessing are implemented to eliminate noise, extraneous data, and duplicates from the dataset. These techniques serve to ascertain the accuracy, consistency, and reliability of the data employed in sentiment analysis.

Another pivotal facet of data quality pertains to the utilization of labeled data. Labeled data refers to data that has been manually annotated with sentiment labels, such as positive, negative, or neutral. This labeled data is instrumental in training and evaluating sentiment analysis models, with the efficacy of these models being contingent upon the quality of the labeled data. To ensure the quality of labeled data, it is imperative to engage a diverse pool of annotators who have received adequate training to consistently and accurately label the data. Additionally, regular quality checks and validation procedures are instrumental in identifying and rectifying any errors or inconsistencies present within the labeled data. In summary, data quality stands as a pivotal determinant of the accuracy and reliability of sentiment analysis outcomes. To safeguard the quality of data employed in sentiment analysis, it is imperative to leverage data cleaning and preprocessing techniques alongside high-quality labeled data. By prioritizing data quality, businesses and organizations can make well-informed decisions based on reliable sentiment analysis results.

Sentiment analysis, as a burgeoning field in NLP and data analytics, has gained substantial attention due to its potential applications in understanding public opinion, market trends, and customer sentiments. However, as sentiment analysis techniques are implemented in diverse contexts, it becomes imperative to address the ethical considerations inherent in this practice, i.e., the key ethical concerns associated with sentiment analysis as summarized below, including biases and limitations, privacy and consent, and the responsible use of sentiment analysis in sensitive domains.

First, sentiment analysis algorithms are susceptible to various biases, both explicit and implicit. Algorithmic bias can emerge from biased training data or inherent biases in the algorithm design, leading to unfair treatment and perpetuation of societal inequalities. Representational bias can arise due to the underrepresentation or misrepresentation of certain demographics or cultural nuances in the training data, resulting in inaccurate sentiment analysis results. Furthermore, sentiment analysis struggles with the interpretation of subtle linguistic cues, such as sarcasm, irony, and context, which may lead to misclassification and distorted sentiment analysis outcomes.

Second, the ethical use of sentiment analysis requires careful consideration of privacy and consent. Sentiment analysis often relies on user-generated content from various sources, such as social media platforms and customer reviews. Collecting and analyzing this data raises concerns regarding data privacy and the need for obtaining informed consent from users. Anonymization and de-identification techniques should be employed to protect user identities and sensitive information. Additionally, ensuring data security and establishing transparent data usage policies are vital in maintaining user trust and upholding ethical standards.

Third, the application of sentiment analysis in sensitive domains, such as healthcare, politics, and legal contexts, demands heightened ethical considerations. In healthcare, for instance, sentiment analysis of patient feedback raises concerns regarding patient privacy, data security, and potential misuse of sensitive health information. Similarly, sentiment analysis in political analysis and public opinion polling must adhere to principles of fairness, impartiality, and transparency to avoid undue influence and manipulation of public sentiment. The potential for emotional manipulation and its impact on psychological well-being should also be acknowledged and addressed responsibly.

Last but not least, fairness and transparency are crucial ethical principles in sentiment analysis. Ensuring fairness entails unbiased algorithm design, representation of diverse perspectives in training data, and monitoring for discriminatory outcomes. Transparency involves providing clear explanations of the sentiment analysis process, including the factors considered and the limitations of the results. Accountability mechanisms should be established to address any ethical violations or misuse of sentiment analysis techniques, including ethical review boards and regulatory bodies overseeing its implementation.

6. Concluding remarks

In conclusion, sentiment analysis has assumed a crucial role for businesses, governments, and individuals in comprehending and responding to public opinion. Nevertheless, there remains considerable scope for enhancing the accuracy and efficacy of sentiment analysis algorithms. The integrated approach, as depicted in **Figure 1**, strives to harness the strengths of different methods while mitigating their respective limitations. Ongoing research and development in this domain are imperative to ensure the continued value and reliability of sentiment analysis. As the volume of available data for analysis continues to expand, sentiment analysis will assume an even greater significance in shaping public opinion and facilitating decision-making processes. Hence, it is imperative for researchers and developers to persist in exploring novel techniques and approaches that enhance the accuracy and effectiveness of sentiment analysis algorithms.

Moreover, sentiment analysis holds potential for application in various fields beyond marketing and public opinion analysis. For instance, it can be deployed in healthcare to analyze patient feedback and enhance the quality of care, or in finance to assess market sentiment and forecast trends. In summary, sentiment analysis is a potent tool with vast potential across diverse domains. Ongoing research and development endeavors are indispensable to ensure its enduring value and reliability for businesses, governments, and individuals alike. Meanwhile, ethical considerations play a pivotal role in the responsible practice of sentiment analysis. Addressing biases and limitations, respecting privacy and consent, and navigating the complexities of sensitive applications are essential for maintaining ethical standards. Fairness, transparency, and accountability should guide the development and deployment of sentiment analysis algorithms, fostering trust, and ensuring that sentiment analysis remains a reliable and valuable tool in an ethically aware and socially responsible manner.

Overall, the 2023 Sentiment Analysis Roadmap kicks off the book Advances in Sentiment Analysis—Techniques, Applications, and Challenges. This introductory chapter constitutes a valuable resource for individuals seeking to comprehend the present state of sentiment analysis and its prospective impact on various industries. It provides a comprehensive overview of the field and offers insights into the future trajectory of sentiment analysis.

Acknowledgements

The editor acknowledges all the contributing authors and reviewers to this book.

Author details

Jinfeng Li
Beijing Institute of Technology, Beijing, China

*Address all correspondence to: jinfengcambridge@bit.edu.cn

References

[1] Jurek A, Mulvenna M, Bi Y. Improved lexicon-based sentiment analysis for social media analytics. Security Informatics. 2015;**4**:9. DOI: 10.1186/s13388-015-0024-x

[2] Julia H, Christopher D. Advances in natural language processing. Science. 2015;**349**(6245):261-266. DOI: 10.1126/science.aaa8685

[3] Guo X, Li J. A novel twitter sentiment analysis model with baseline correlation for financial market prediction with improved efficiency. In: Proceedings of the Sixth IEEE International Conference on Social Networks Analysis, Management and Security (SNAMS); 22-25 October 2019; Granada, Spain. New York: IEEE; 2019. pp. 472-477. DOI: 10.1109/SNAMS.2019.8931720

[4] Wankhade M, Rao A, Kulkarni C. A survey on sentiment analysis methods, applications, and challenges. Artificial Intelligence Review. 2022;**55**:5731-5780. DOI: 10.1007/s10462-022-10144-1

[5] Asghar M, Khan A, Ahmad S, Qasim M, Khan I. Lexicon-enhanced sentiment analysis framework using rule-based classification scheme. PLoS One. 2017;**12**(2):e0171649. DOI: 10.1371/journal.pone.0171649

Section 2

Advanced Techniques

Chapter 2

Preprocessing of Slang Words for Sentiment Analysis on Public Perceptions in Twitter

Media Anugerah Ayu and Abdul Haris Muhendra

Abstract

Nowadays, many people express their evaluations on certain issues *via* social media freely, which makes huge amounts of data generated every day on social media. On Twitter, public opinions are diverse, which makes them possible to be processed for sentiment analysis. However, many people conveniently use slang words in expressing their opinions on Twitter. These slang words in the text can sometimes lead to miscalculation of language processing due to the absence of the "real words." This research aimed to investigate the effect of adding slang words as part of the preprocessing stage to the performance of the conducted sentiment analysis. The sentiment analysis was performed using Naïve Bayes Classifier as the classification algorithm with term frequency-inverse document frequency (TF-IDF) as the feature extraction. The research focused on comparing the performance of the conducted sentiment analysis on data that was preprocessed using slang dictionary and the ones that did not use slang dictionary. The case used in this research was texts related to COVID-19 pandemic in Indonesia, especially the ones related to the implementation of vaccines. The performance evaluation results indicate that sentiment analysis of data preprocessed using slang word dictionary has shown better accuracy than the ones preprocessed without it.

Keywords: sentiment analysis, slang words, social media, performance evaluation, public opinions, Naïve Bayes, Twitter

1. Introduction

The rapid growth of the Internet nowadays has made huge amounts of information spread through different platforms, such as blog posts, online discussion forums, product websites, social media, and so forth. Several tools/applications are used, in the form of social media, as the basis for people to communicate and share their opinion or information with different methods such as texts, images, videos, audios, and so on. One of the popular social media that are capable of gathering information and opinion from general people is Twitter. Twitter is one of the 10 most-visited websites that have been used as a platform to collect data; for example, it is used to collect the tweets related to the candidate for election [1, 2]. Using several unique features such as hashtags and retweets can make data collection easier. The collected data then is analyzed to see whether the opinion goes toward positive, negative, or neutral sentiment. Sentiment analysis or opinion mining is one of the methods of text mining to determine the attitude of a subject toward a certain topic [2, 3]. Many studies have been done with a different approach. In their work, Bouazizi and Ohtsuki [4] approached the work by proposing multi-class classification sentiment analysis, while [5] approached the work by comparing the preprocessing method in sentiment analysis. Sentiment analysis requires the classification of the tweets that have been collected, toward the determination of its positive, negative, or neutral review.

Classification is a process or technique of categorizing different sets of data into different classes [1]. There are two techniques for classifying the data, which are lexicon based and machine learning. The lexicon-based approach works by classifying the sentiment based on the dictionary that has been provided beforehand. The dictionary contains a large amount of data, where each of them is labeled by annotators, either manually or automatically. On the other hand, machine learning uses training and testing data to predict the output in classifying the data. Some of the examples use common algorithms like Naïve Bayes, Maximum Entropy, Support Vector Machine, and K-means for classification.

In machine learning, Naïve Bayes is one of the most commonly used techniques for classification. Naïve Bayes works best when used on a well-formed text corpus. Corpus is a collection of documents with a large number of total documents. This means that the algorithm will use training data as a way to learn the input data given and make decisions from it. The decision is then divided into three sentiments, which are positive, negative, and neutral sentiments. In this research, the Naïve Bayes algorithm has been assessed for finding accuracy, precision, recall, and F-measure.

Out of many specific kinds of sentiment analysis that have been conducted, assessing sarcasm is regarded as one of the hardest challenges to explore, especially in Indonesia where research on that area is limited. Sarcasm or irony can also be a burden on the performance of sentiment analysis [6]. Another issue in Indonesia is that a popular way to type a tweet is by using slang words or abbreviations. Singh and Kumari [7] stated that slang is one of the major challenges in this area other than noise, relevance, emoticons, and folksonomies. Disambiguation because of the ignorance of the slang sometimes leads to miscalculation of the sentiment. Some researchers have done research optimizing the data cleaning when the slang word occurs in the document. In Indonesia, some researchers such as [6, 8, 9] specifically focus on the slang word in their paper. The method used in their paper varies, from improving the stemming process for the slang to generating their slang lexicon. Using one of the basic stemming algorithms for the Indonesian language, evaluating the sentiment can be done better in terms of accuracy. The common method for the Indonesian language stemming is by using Nazief and Adriani Stemming Algorithm [10]. Some other research studies, such as Drus and Khalid [1], Jianqiang and Xiaolin [5], Rahayu et al. [6], Nuritha et al. [11], Adarsh and Ravikumar [12], Ferdiana et al. [13], Fitri et al. [14], Mandloi and Patel [15], show the effectiveness of term frequency-inverse document frequency (TF-IDF) from the lexicon-based approach as feature extraction, while Naïve Bayes is the optimum classification from machine learning approach.

One interesting case for sentiment analysis to be done in Indonesia is the topic regarding the coronavirus (COVID-19) pandemic. Over a year of pandemic events throughout the world, Indonesia had become the country with the highest case prevalence and fatality rate among Southeast Asia countries. By checking the trending tweets that are discussing the virus on Twitter, hashtags related to it, such as "#covid", "#covid19", "#delta", "#omicron", "#vaccine". Social and physical distancing to reduce the transmission of the virus had been implemented in several countries, including Indonesia. The campaign to limit human-to-human transmission as well as self-hygiene was required to be done. After more than a year of the first case of coronavirus in Indonesia, positive cases in Indonesia had risen with a total of 4,763,252 as of 12 February 2022. The government had taken action to apply the coronavirus vaccine to help reduce the spread of the virus. Up until 12 February 2022, 135,209,233 people of Indonesia had been given fully dosed vaccine, which is 50.7% of the population.

Observing the sentiment of people talking about the virus may become one of the measurements to see if people's perceptions toward global pandemic can be used to measure the emotion of the people in relation to the pandemic. Therefore, one of the objectives of this research is to help in concluding the temporary result of the perception of Indonesian people toward pandemic. The main objective of this research study is to seek a better result of sentiment analysis if the slang words and abbreviations that are commonly used in tweets can be considered in the process. The data collection and processing will be retrieved from Twitter API. The selected sentiment of people's opinion on Twitter can be done by choosing several popular words related to COVID-19 and its vaccination. The collected data are then processed into two different stages, one that uses slang word and abbreviation dictionary while the other one does not use slang word and abbreviation dictionary in the preprocessing step. Evaluation then will be done by comparing the performance measure of both processes, the one with slang words included and the one without.

The remainder of this paper is structured as follows: Section 2 describes the related work from previous study and Section 3 discusses the method used in this research. Section 4 presents result from preliminary research and the main experiments and their discussions. Section 5 discusses the conclusion.

2. Related work

This section discusses previous studies done that are related to this research study. The discussed studies are grouped into four, that is, studies related to public perception, sentiment analysis, Twitter, and COVID-19.

2.1 Public perception

Public opinion/perception refers to the social and political attitudes held by the public toward the emergence, spread, and change of social events in a certain social space. It can be expressed according to entities, behaviors, and emotional words. Previous research has been conducted on many branches of the topic of assessing public perception.

Assessing public perceptions is usually conducted through the use of surveys, including defined preference or customer satisfaction surveys. Casas and Delmelle [16] discussed how Twitter can be a method to assess public perceptions of BRT (bus rapid transit) in area of Cali, Colombia. The main purpose of their research was that they wanted to know what discussion is happening in terms of transportation systems, especially on the topic of user satisfaction and/or service quality. Moreover, they wanted to ensure that the information of tweets in the Latin American context is similar to the knowledge about the quality factors in the country. They used Twitter

Search API, twitterSearch library, within a 9-day time frame, which was filtered by geographic location within a 60 km radius from the center of Cali city. Moreover, they only filtered two search keywords of tweets: MetroCali and MIO.

While other research used public perception to understand user satisfaction of public transportation in a city, public perception can be also used as a way to get crowdsourcing information in disasters, for example, in getting information of building seismic safety following the Canterbury earthquakes in New Zealand [17]. The purpose of their research is close to this research, which is related to the topic of a nation-level disaster of coronavirus 2019, which seeks for risk and expert opinion to relieve public anxiety and acceptance of building standards regarding the durability to withstand earthquakes.

In terms of social media itself, many researchers discuss it more specifically, especially when talking about public opinion with social media data. Klašnja et al. [18], in part of Oxford Handbooks Online, discussed social media data and public opinion. They stated three factors of why social media can be used to measure public opinion. First, social media offers a chance to observe the opinions of the public without any prompting or framing effects from analysts. It means that the analyst does not need any other burdensome environment or deciding a topic from the analyst's view; rather we can observe them by choosing what the analyst wants and filtering all of the related opinions. The second factor is the reach of their data. Since social media can be found all over the world, they provide tons of data on a daily or even hourly basis. Twitter itself is likely already the biggest time series dataset of individual public opinion available to the public. Third and the last factor is cost and practicality. With a few codes executed in a simple device, anyone can capture a selected topic in real time for free. These three factors are the main reasons why social media is considered to be a good choice for examining public opinion.

2.2 Sentiment analysis

Sentiment analysis or opinion mining is the study of determining people's perspective of opinion, attitude, and emotion into something related to them, such as entities, individuals, issues, events, or topics [2, 3]. Its focus is to analyze opinions from a text document. It is part of natural language processing (NLP), which is a technique for analyzing and describing text naturally. The study involves classifying the attitude of texts into three common parts, which are a positive, negative, and neutral statement. To classify the different sentiment methods, various algorithms were developed.

In their paper, Drus and Khalid [1] present a systematic literature review (SLR) of sentiment analysis topic. Taken from five online resource databases that publish literature, which are Emerald Insight, Science Direct, Association for Computing Machinery (ACM), Scopus, and IEEE, they identified a total search of 407 articles with keywords "Sentiment analysis, social media, Facebook, Twitter" during publish time between 2014 and February 2019. After screening the available articles, a total of 24 articles are selected. Out of 24 papers, 7 papers used lexicon-based methods, 10 papers used machine learning methods, and 7 papers showed the combination of both methods. Another paper [2] also conducted an SLR on sentiment analysis that focused on Twitter data. Out of 42 papers deeply reviewed, 23 used machine learning-based approaches, 10 employed lexicon-based approaches, and 9 papers used hybrid-based ones.

2.2.1 Lexicon-based approach

Lexicon is one of the methods to approach sentiment analysis, which does not require any training data but only depends on the dictionary that has been prepared before. Lexicon-based approach is included as an unsupervised learning method [1]. The lexicon-based method works by determining the overall sentiment tendency of a given text by utilizing a pre-established lexicon of words weighted with their sentiment orientation or dictionary. It works by identifying the final polarity score of the given text from prepared language resources of positive, negative, and neutral words.

Many papers have discussed using the lexicon method to get the sentiment of people's opinions. In their work, Al-Thubaity et al. [19] create their lexicon by using the dataset of Saudi Dialect Twitter Corpus (SDTC) that consists of 5400 tweets containing Saudi dialect. The corpus was chosen to minimize the risk of dataset prejudice against a specific topic. Then, the tweet classification is done using SaudiSenti, which is a lexicon containing 4431 words. The lexicon is then compared with the previous lexicon available AraSenTi with the result that SaudiSenti outperformed AraSenti when comparing neutral tweets. Mukhtar et al. [20] works on a lexicon-based approach in the Urdu language. The method used is to first create a Sentiment Lexicon in the Urdu language with the help of annotators; then, the analyzer is created to perform sentiment analysis. Even though they use the lexicon approach, some machine learning approaches are still in use, such as stop word removal, sentences classification, and attribute selection. The result is that the lexicon-based approach outperforms the machine learning approach in many aspects, such as accuracy, precision, recall, F-measure, time taken, and effort. This can happen because the lexicon and the analyzer are well-developed.

Besides being used to get the sentiment, the lexicon can also be used to collect other things, such as a slang dictionary. Wu et al. [21], Salsabila et al. [22] and Muliady and Widiputra [23] discussed the context of making a slang dictionary. The crawled slang words are retrieved by the online dictionary in their respective language, and some provide them with a sentiment score beside the meaning and choose most of them to avoid mistakes.

2.2.2 Machine learning approach

According to Vieira et al. [24], machine learning is "an area of artificial intelligence that is concerned with identifying patterns from data and using these patterns to make a prediction about unseen data." It involves learning patterns in the data, storing the processed patterns, and then making them as a method to do predictions. It differs from a traditional statistic in at least four ways: it has a capability of speculating at the individual level; it focuses on maximizing generalizability; it is a data-driven approach; it takes into account individual heterogeneity. Based on the category of machine learning, supervised learning is by far the most commonly used approach in research that requires machine learning. Supervised learning is a machine learning algorithm where prepared correlations between data and expected outcomes are provided as examples [25]. It uses the algorithm to learn the optimal function that occupies the relationship between the input and the variable.

Taking an example, the learning process can be compared with student learning with a teacher. The teacher knows the correct answers to some questions, and the student tries to answer the questions as close to the correct answers as possible. If the student happens to get the wrong answers, the teacher corrects the mistake. It means the process of predicting the result with the difference of the predictions and target should be as small as possible. A supervised method works based on training classifiers by using combinations of features, for example: in tweet context, the information features can be in the form of hashtags, retweet, emoticon, capital words, and so forth [26]. It works by utilizing algorithms to extract and detect sentiment from data with the most commonly used algorithm: Naïve Bayes, Support Vector Machine, and Random Forest.

Work presented in Singh et al. [27] performs Twitter sentiment analysis using the Rapid Miner tool. The author uses two common algorithms, Naïve Bayes and k-NN algorithms. The dataset was fetched from Twitter with the topic of government campaign and ready to be classified into positive and negative opinions. Both common algorithms Naïve Bayes and K-NN perform with 100% accuracy to find positive values but fail to find negative values. The author suggests using a tool other than the Rapid Miner tool, which is the NLTK toolkit from Python since it consists of many sources of inbuilt libraries.

2.3 Twitter

Twitter is one of the famous social media that allow users to post brief text updates, with one tweet (text message) limited to 280 characters. The official release of this microblogging service was on 13 July 2006, which can be accessed *via* web or mobile [14]. With over 313 million monthly active users and over 500 million tweets per day, Twitter has become one of the most promising platforms to enhance the social, political, or economic side of individuals or organizations [5].

Many interesting features have made Twitter popular as a data source for many studies related to public opinions. With limitation for 280 characters, users only need to spend a little time creating one tweet. Moreover, properties like "ReTweet" make spreading information become so much faster. Users only need to click or tap the retweet icon (described as a double arrow sign that creates a loop) to make the tweet appear on their homepage. Hashtag (labeled by the sign "#") usage is also making people find the topic easily. According to Bouazizi and Ohtsuki [28], hashtags are "labels used on social network and microblogging services which make it easier for users to find messages with a specific theme or content." It is useful not only to spread news or discussion to refer to the topics being discussed but also to set a trending topic. Another uniqueness of Twitter is that the data provided can be accessed freely by using the Twitter API, thus making the data easier to collect. By registering for Twitter Developer, collecting and processing the data can be done without the need to do anything that breaks the rules.

Various studies have used Twitter as their data source in doing sentiment analysis. Work presented in Drus and Khalid [1] has reviewed 24 papers related to sentiment analysis, whereby only 6 of them did not use Twitter as their context, rather using other sources, such as YouTube, Facebook, Stock Twits, or news blog. Another work presented in Wang et al. [2] has reviewed 42 papers using Twitter as their data source for conducting sentiment analysis. A study by Zimmer and Proferes [29] shows a topology of Twitter research over 380 academic publications ranged from 2006 to 2012 that used Twitter as their main platform of data collection and analysis. Furthermore, a recent study presented in [30] has also been based on Twitter data to develop a sentiment analysis model in relation to stock market price.

2.4 COVID-19

It is mentioned in Harapan et al. [31] that the coronavirus was first identified as a cold in 1960, which was treated as a simple nonfatal virus. It was known as COVID-19 when the first case was identified at Wuhan, China, in December 2019. Later, a new type of coronavirus 2019-nCoV was found from the outbreak in Wuhan. WHO declared that this is a global pandemic on 11 March 2020 since it affected 172 out of 195 countries with more than 30,000 reported deaths. The way the coronavirus spread generally was through airborne droplets. People can get the infection if one of the following body parts is in contact with the infected droplet: eyes, nose, or mouth. The effect causes respiratory infection including pneumonia, cold, sneezing, and coughing [32].

The strategy to reduce the spread of the virus is by doing simple practices; covering the mouth and nose while coughing or sneezing, maintaining a minimum of 1-m distance between persons, and frequent handwashing just postpone the virus from spreading. The movement of "social distancing" was being held in many countries that listed containing positive cases, with the strategies of closing any educational institutions and workplaces, canceling any event that required mass gatherings, self-quarantining people who were suspected with the contact of the virus, stay-at-home recommendations, and even lockdown in some cities [33]. Self-quarantine of people with symptoms of this virus is because the incubation period of the virus is 14 days or less with an average of 5 days [34]. Hence, the facilities still open even in this outbreak need to check common symptoms that people have. Every facility needs to be equipped with at least a thermal detector and hand sanitizer.

A study presented in Nicola et al. [35] reviewed the pandemic in terms of socio-economic aspects. The classification is divided into three sectors: primary sectors, which are industries that consist of raw materials; secondary sectors, producing complete products; and tertiary sectors, including service providers. We can see that there is an important missing part, which is social impact. Lockdown in many countries had increased the level of problems in domestic violence and physical, emotional, and sexual abuse. Many instances have been found that it is more difficult to expose domestic violence since no one can leave their house if it is not necessary. Thus, the guideline to find and report domestic abuse can be found in several media. Vieira et al. [33] talks about how to treat well-being during the pandemic. Stress is one of the unavoidable effects of lockdown due to limited activity that can be done. The author suggests that people need to be aware of this pandemic to prevent the risk of health problems due to stress. Updating on the situation needs to be done daily on reliable sources of information. Misinformation among news should be reduced by using more diverse channels such as television, radio, newspaper, and online news. Information should be spread out in ways that people understand what they need to do.

Another study in Chen et al. [36] has focused on retrieving public opinion from one of the popular news websites with keywords related to the topic of coronavirus, ranging from 1 January 2020 to 7 July 2020. By using a skip-gram model of word to vector and manual screening, the filtered trigger words are selected as the dataset. They construct a relationship between the dominant public opinion by analyzing the frequency and probability of keywords in each category.

3. Methodology

As mentioned earlier, this study aims to investigate the effect of including a step with slang word dictionary in the preprocessing phase of the tweet-data to the performance of the conducted sentiment analysis. The dataset is retrieved by crawling tweets with related keywords on Twitter. The search query used to get the twitter is related to the topic of COVID-19 in Indonesia, such as "corona," "covid-19," "vaksin", as well as the hashtags related to it, such as "#vaccine," "#vaksin," and "#corona". The tweets data were taken every day, which was limited to 7 days (1 week) from the day of execution. After that, the data would be stored as a CSV file, which will be used to get the sentiment score. The scoring of the sentiment would be held automatically using the Indonesian lexicon approach that is available on Github.

To be able to get Twitter datasets, we need to create a Twitter developer account. Apps of the developer are also needed to generate the key and token. There are four keys to getting access to data collection: Access token, access token secret, consumer key, and consumer key secret. These keys will be used to crawl the tweets legally *via* Twitter API. The dictionary for slang words is retrieved from other work, which are Okky Ibrohim's slang word dictionaries [37] that can be found in GitHub (link), Louis Owen's in GitHub (link), and Rama Prakoso's in Github (link). This dictionary later will be used in preprocessing part of the slang word process or usually called normalization.

Later on, the dataset from the crawling process will be divided into two parts, which are training data and testing data. The training data will be labeled with positive, negative, or neutral sentiment before being applied to the classification process. When the data has been labeled and trained into the classification process, the testing data will be applied to the process as the data that will be evaluated. This process is repeated once again but with different treatment from the last time. The first treatment will be without slang word dictionary as the base compared to the other experiment. The other experiment will use the combination of the slang dictionary mentioned above as the treatment. The details of the research process can be seen in **Figure 1**.

Figure 1 shows the research model of sentiment analysis, and the process was divided into four different processes to make it easier. In the beginning, the data was collected from Twitter through API credentials. The collected data were stored in a database in a corpus type file (.csv) and then moved to the preprocessing stage to read tweets. The preprocessing stage was divided into two, which in the first method did not use slang word and abbreviation dictionary, while the second method used it. The Python library is called "Sastrawi," which allows the words in the Indonesian language (Bahasa Indonesia) to be reduced into their base form (stemming). The results were labeled by using the TextBlob library of Python language. The training set and the testing set were processed for the feature extraction; then, the model was evaluated based on the result given. Otherwise, the error was prompted when the machine learning algorithm fails to predict the sentiment. In the end, by looking for both accuracy and error, this study can conclude the result of the tweets.

3.1 Data preprocessing

Steps done in the preprocessing phase of this research are: case folding, cleansing, converting negation, converting emoticon, tokenization, stop words removal, and stemming. The difference between process one and two is the additional slang word and abbreviation dictionary that is applied before the stemming process. Methods to do the preprocessing are listed in **Figure 1** as well.

Case folding is a step where all the uppercase letters in the tweeted document will be converted to lowercase. The only word from "a" to "z" that accepted in this stage. The purpose is to remove the data redundancy where the difference is only from the letter. Next, cleansing is done to clean the words that do not correlate with the result

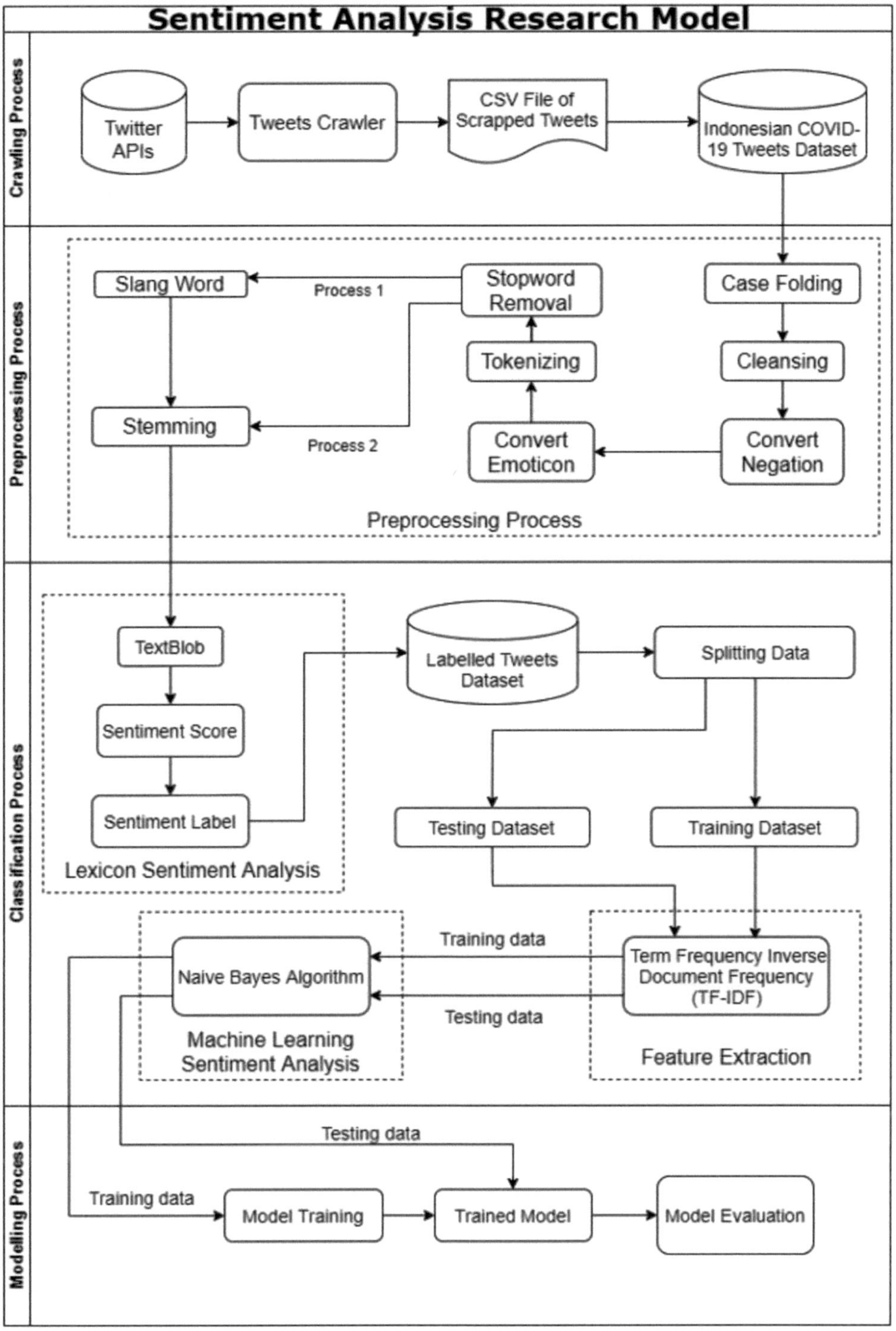

Figure 1.
Process flow of the sentiment analysis with slang words.

of sentiment classification. The component of the tweeted document has various attributes that do not affect the sentiment since every tweet mostly has those attributes. Examples of unimportant attributes of tweets are: the mention feature (symbolized by "@"), hashtag (symbolized by "#"), link (symbolized by "http," "b it.ly," and ".com"), and character (~!@#$%^&*()_ + {}[]|?<>;':). These attributes will be replaced by a space ""character to make it easier to be classified. Then, the process to convert negation word that exists in a tweet. This negation will change the sentiment value of the document; thus, the negation word will be combined with the next word. Examples of negation words are "bukan," "jangan," "tidak," and so forth. It is then followed by convert emoticon, which removes every emoticon from the text. Examples of emoticon are ("😊", "😐", "😟", "😉", "😊").

The next process is tokenizing, which cuts every word and arranges it into a single piece. The word in the document is the word that is separated by space. The result of this process is a single word for weighting. Then, stop word removal is performed to remove the word that is not suitable for the document topic, in which the word does not affect the accuracy of sentiment classification. The removed words will be stored in the stop word database. If in the document, there are stop words, then it will be replaced by a space character. Then, the process with slang words which is the main part of the research. By comparing this additional process and the one without it in terms of performance, the comparison can be analyzed. This process is done by changing the word that is not following the Indonesian standard word (EYD, "Ejaan yang Disempurnakan") referring to the slang word dictionary used. After that, stemming is done to convert the words in a document to be back to their root by using certain rules. The process of Indonesian language stemming is done by removing suffix, prefix, and confix, on the document.

3.2 Feature extraction with TF-IDF

TF-IDF is one of the methods commonly used in feature extraction. This method is famous for being efficient, easy, and accurate. It is used to calculate the weight of the words used in information retrieval. It calculates the value of TF and IDF on every token (words) in every document in the corpus.

TF is the amount of word occurrence in a document. The more a word appears in a document, the more it affects the document. Otherwise, the less a word appears in a document, the less it affects the document. IDF is word weighting that is based on how much a document contains a certain word. The more a document contains a certain word, the less the word affects the document. Otherwise, the less a document contains a certain word, the more the word affects the document. The equation to determine TF-IDF can be found below:

$$\mathrm{IDF}\ (\mathrm{w}) = \log\left(\frac{N}{\mathrm{DF}(\mathrm{w})}\right) \tag{1}$$

$$\mathrm{TF}-\mathrm{IDF}\ (\mathrm{w}, \mathrm{d}) = \mathrm{TF}(\mathrm{w}, \mathrm{d}) \times \mathrm{IDF}(\mathrm{W}) \tag{2}$$

Where IDF(w) is the inverse document frequency of word W, N is the number of documents, DF(w) is the number of documents containing word W, TF-IDF(w,d) is the weight of a words in all document, TF(w,d) is the frequency of word W occurrence in document, and W is a word and d is a document.

3.3 Classification with Naïve Bayes algorithm

In this paper, the algorithm used for the classification process is the Naïve Bayes algorithm. The algorithm was chosen because it is simple and can perform well with a small dataset, which will be useful for classifying positive and negative words that are conditionally independent of each other. Depending on the probability model, this classifier can be trained to run the supervised learning effectively. The algorithm is derived from the classifier that is based on the appearance or absence of class A in a given document B. The following is the basis formula used in Naïve Bayes algorithm:

$$P(\mathrm{A}|\mathrm{B}) = \frac{P(\mathrm{A})P(\mathrm{B}|\mathrm{A})}{P(\mathrm{B})} \tag{3}$$

Where A belongs to a positive or negative class and B belongs to the document whose class is being predicted. The numerator ($P(\mathrm{A})$ and $P(\mathrm{B}|\mathrm{A})$ was obtained during data training. It represents every tweet in attribute $(a_1, a_2, a_3, \dots, a_\mathrm{n})$ where a_1 is the first word, a_2 is the second, and so on, where V represents the class set. When the classification begins, this method will create a category or class with the highest probability (V_{MAP}) by inserting attributes $(a_1, a_2, a_3, \dots, a_\mathrm{n})$. The equation is given below:

$$V_{\mathrm{MAP}} = \underset{v_j \in v}{\mathrm{argmax}} P(v_j|a_1, a_2, a_3, \dots a_n) \tag{4}$$

By using Bayes theorem, Eq. (4) can be written as:

$$V_{\mathrm{MAP}} = \underset{v_j \in v}{\mathrm{argmax}} P\frac{(a_1, a_2, a_3, \dots a_n|V_j)P(V_j)}{P(a_1, a_2, a_3, \dots a_n)} \tag{5}$$

$P(a_1, a_2, a_3, \dots, a_n)$ becomes constant for every v_j; thus, the equation can be declared by Eq. (6) as below:

$$V_{\mathrm{MAP}} = \underset{v_j \in v}{\mathrm{argmax}} P\ (v_j|a_1, a_2, a_3, \dots a_n)P(V_j) \tag{6}$$

Naïve Bayes Classifier simplifies this by assuming that in every category, each attribute is conditionally independent of each other. Thus:

$$P(a_1, a_2, a_3, \dots a_n|V_j) = \prod_i P(a_i|v_j) \tag{7}$$

Then, by substituting Eq. (6) to Eq. (7), it will create a formula (8) as below:

$$V_{\mathrm{MAP}} = \underset{vj \in V}{\mathrm{argmax}} P(v_j) \times \prod_i P(a_i|v_j) \tag{8}$$

$P(v_j)$ and probability of word a_i for every category, $P(a_i|v_j)$ will be calculated at training process based on the following formulas (9) and (10):

$$(v_j) = \frac{\mathrm{docs}_j}{\mathrm{training}} \tag{9}$$

$$P(a_i|v_j) = \frac{n_i + 1}{n + \text{vocabulary}} \tag{10}$$

Where $docs_j$ is the sum of a document in category j and training is the sum of documents used in the training process, while n_i is the amount of appearance of word a_i in category v_j, n is the amount of vocabulary that appears in category v_j, and vocabulary is the number of unique words on every training data.

3.4 Design of experiments

There are two phases of experiments conducted in this research, which are preliminary works and main experiments. In the preliminary research, we did experiments by looking at several variables, which are the effect of using slang dictionaries, and the other one is the splitting of training and testing data to different ratios. **Table 1** shows the design of experiments (DoEs) for preliminary research. For the experiment, the data used was from 4000 tweets crawled on 14 July 2021. The slang word dictionary used for the preliminary works was dictionary A (Okky Ibrohim), which generates six results for the preliminary works. The results were then analyzed to choose which data splitting is going to be used in the main experiments.

The main experiments were then conducted with different parameters involved, which are various slang word dictionaries. There were eight different experiments conducted as presented in **Table 2**.

4. Result and discussion

This section presents the results and discussions from two phases of the research study, that is, preliminary works and main experiments.

		Slang word dictionary	
		Using slang dictionary	**Not using slang dictionary**
Data splitting	60:40	Experiment 1	Experiment 4
	70:30	Experiment 2	Experiment 5
	80:20	Experiment 3	Experiment 6

Table 1.
DoEs for preliminary research.

Main experiment	Slang word dictionary	Main experiment	Slang word dictionary
Experiment 1	No slang dictionary	Experiment 5	Dictionary A and B
Experiment 2	Dictionary A	Experiment 6	Dictionary A and C
Experiment 3	Dictionary B	Experiment 7	Dictionary B and C
Experiment 4	Dictionary C	Experiment 8	Dictionary A, B, and C

Table 2.
DoEs for the main experiment.

4.1 Preliminary works

The preliminary work was conducted with tweets crawled using Python script to get query by limiting the search area within a 50 km radius from the central geocode of Jakarta, Indonesia. **Table 3** shows the example of first five results of the raw crawled data.

Preprocessing stage was then conducted to the scrapped tweets. As explained in the methodology section, the preprocessing was done to clean the data to ease and simplify further process. Two types of preprocessing were performed: (i) tweets were cleaned without using slang word dictionary and (ii) tweets were cleaned using slang word dictionary. **Table 4** shows the results from both preprocessing channels, respectively. It can be observed that there are some differences in the number of words that are not covered when not using slang dictionary.

Next, results from the preprocessing stage were labeled using a lexicon-based approach, which retrieved from the number of words containing the sentiment value and scored it based on the dictionary of positive and negative words. The scoring of sentiment is divided into three, which are positive for a score above 0, negative for a score below 0, and neutral for a score exactly 0. **Tables 5** and **6** show the results of the first five tweets that have been labeled with lexicon-based approach.

Created at	Text	Location	Username	Language
2021–07–14 14:31:21	@ridwanhr @msaid_didu Innalillahiwainnalilahirajiuun Ada kah data2 org yg minggal covid ini sdh divaskin atau blm? Kalau ada brp org sdh vaksin yg mninggal terhitung dari vaksinasi ini di mulai, klo mau detail merk vaksin nya skalian	Jakarta	ndra_833	in
2021–07–14 14:30:52	@BeBuzzerNKRI Dampaknya juga gak signifikan vaksin GR individu karena jumlahnya sedikit. Tapi ekses kecemburuan sosialnya begitu besar. Ekses ini yang bisa membuat penjaga kedai kopi, semir sepatu dan pedagang kecil lainnya terbakar emosinya. Kalau mau berdampak, perusahaan kepada pekerja.	Jakarta	Uki23	in
2021–07–14 14:30:06	Vaksin Covid-19 baru bisa diberikan untuk anak berusia 12-17 tahun. Meski demikian, ada beberapa cara untuk menjaga imunitas anak yang belum divaksin. https://t.co/70tG0Dhbe4	Jakarta	kompascom	in
2021–07–14 14:29:49	@detikinet @detikinet bahas dunk apa boleh yg disuntik vaksin merekam video saat penyuntikan vaksin Karena ada beberapa video yg nakes bilang tidak boleh merekam saat proses vaksin Di satu sisi merekam proses vaksin bisa jadi bukti penyuntikan sesuai SOP & sesuai dosis Cc @KemenkesRI @PBIDI	Jakarta	ari_aditya	in
2021–07–14 14:29:29	Pak pres. @jokowi mohon pak dibuat peraturan saja wajib pakai sertifikat vaksin untuk semua layanan transportasi. Pasti org yg anti vaksin itu akhirnya minta divaksin.	Jakarta	Yehezkiel_Sound	in

Table 3.
The first five results of crawled tweets.

With slang word dictionary	Without slang word dictionary
innalillahiwainnalilahirajiuun kah data2 orang minggal covid sdh divaskin orang sdh vaksin tinggal hitung vaksinasi detail merk vaksin	innalillahiwainnalilahirajiuun kah data2 org yg minggal covid sdh divaskin blm brp org sdh vaksin yg mninggal hitung vaksinasi klo detail merk vaksin skalian
dampak signifikan vaksin gede individu ekses cemburu sosial ekses jaga kedai kopi semir sepatu dagang bakar emosi dampak usaha kerja	dampak gak signifikan vaksin gr individu ekses cemburu sosial ekses jaga kedai kopi semir sepatu dagang bakar emosi dampak usaha kerja
vaksin covid 19 anak usia 12 17 jaga imunitas anak vaksin	vaksin covid 19 anak usia 12 17 jaga imunitas anak vaksin
bahas dunk suntik vaksin rekam video sunti vaksin video tenaga sehat bilang rekam proses vaksin sisi rekam proses vaksin bukti sunti sesuai sop amp sesuai dosis cc pbidi	bahas dunk yg suntik vaksin rekam video sunti vaksin video yg nakes bilang rekam proses vaksin sisi rekam proses vaksin bukti sunti sesuai sop amp sesuai dosis cc pbidi
pres mohon atur wajib pakai sertifikat vaksin layan transportasi orang anti vaksin vaksin	pres mohon atur wajib pakai ifikat vaksin layan transpo asi org yg anti vaksin vaksin

Table 4.
Results from cleaning process of the first five tweets.

Text	Tokenized words	Polarity score	Polarity
innalillahiwainnalilahirajiuun kah data2 orang minggal covid sdh divaskin orang sdh vaksin tinggal hitung vaksinasi detail merk vaksin	["innalillahiwainnalilahirajiuun," "kah," "data2," "orang," "minggal," "covid," "sdh," "divaskin," "orang," sdh," vaksin," "tinggal," "hitung," "vaksinasi," "detail," "merk," "vaksin"]	1	Positive
dampak signifikan vaksin gede individu ekses cemburu sosial ekses jaga kedai kopi semir sepatu dagang bakar emosi dampak usaha kerja	["dampak," "signifikan," "vaksin," "gede," "individu," "ekses," "cemburu," sosial," "ekses," "jaga," "kedai," "kopi," "semir," "sepatu," "dagang," "bakar," "emosi," "dampak," "usaha," "kerja"]	−9	Negative
vaksin covid 19 anak usia 12 17 jaga imunitas anak vaksin	["vaksin," "covid," "19," "anak," "usia," "12," "17," "jaga," "imunitas," "anak," "vaksin"]	−7	Negative
bahas dunk suntik vaksin rekam video sunti vaksin video tenaga sehat bilang rekam proses vaksin sisi rekam proses vaksin bukti sunti sesuai sop amp sesuai dosis cc pbidi	["bahas," "dunk," "suntik," "vaksin," "rekam," "video," "sunti," "vaksin," "video," "tenaga," "sehat," "bilang," "rekam," "proses," "vaksin," "sisi," "rekam," "proses," "vaksin," "bukti," "sunti," "sesuai," "sop," "amp," "sesuai," "dosis," "cc," "pbidi"]	10	Positive
pres mohon atur wajib pakai sertifikat vaksin layan transportasi orang anti vaksin vaksin	["pres," "mohon," "atur," "wajib," "pakai," "sertifikat," "vaksin," "layan," "transportasi," "orang," "anti," "vaksin," "vaksin"]	−4	Negative

Table 5.
First five tweets tokenized and labeled using slang word dictionary.

The results of tokenizing the tweets show differences between the ones with slang word dictionary and the ones without. This can make different results of calculations when the feature extraction process is applied. This propagates to the differences in polarity score, even though the polarity labels are all the same.

Text	Tokenized words	Polarity score	Polarity
innalillahiwainnalilahirajiuun kah data2 org yg minggal covid sdh divaskin blm brp org sdh vaksin yg mninggal hitung vaksinasi klo detail merk vaksin skalian	["innalillahiwainnalilahirajiuun," "kah," "data2," "org," "yg," "minggal," "covid," sdh," "divaskin," "blm," "brp," "org," "sdh," "vaksin," "yg," "mninggal," "hitung," "vaksinasi," "klo," "detail," "merk," "vaksin," "skalian"]	3	Positive
dampak gak signifikan vaksin gr individu ekses cemburu sosial ekses jaga kedai kopi semir sepatu dagang bakar emosi dampak usaha kerja	["dampak," "gak," "signifikan," "vaksin," "gr," "individu," "ekses," "cemburu," "sosial," "ekses," "jaga," "kedai," "kopi," "semir," "sepatu," "dagang," "bakar," "emosi," "dampak," "usaha," "kerja"]	−9	Negative
vaksin covid 19 anak usia 12 17 jaga imunitas anak vaksin	["vaksin," "covid," "19," "anak," "usia," "12," '17," "jaga," "imunitas," "anak," "vaksin"]	−7	Negative
bahas dunk yg suntik vaksin rekam video sunti vaksin video yg nakes bilang rekam proses vaksin sisi rekam proses vaksin bukti sunti sesuai sop amp sesuai dosis cc pbidi	["bahas," "dunk," "yg," "suntik," "vaksin," "rekam," "video," "sunti," "vaksin," "video," "yg," "nakes," "bilang," "rekam," "proses," "vaksin," "sisi," "rekam," "proses," "vaksin," "bukti," "sunti," "sesuai," "sop," "amp," "sesuai," "dosis," "cc," "pbidi"]	4	Positive
pres mohon atur wajib pakai ifikat vaksin layan transpo asi org yg anti vaksin vaksin	["pres," "mohon," "atur," "wajib," "pakai," "ifikat," "vaksin," "layan," "transpo," "asi," "org," "yg," "anti," 'vaksin," "vaksin"]	−4	Negative

Table 6.
First five tweets tokenized and labeled without slang word dictionary.

Figure 2 shows the sentiment distribution of the tweets dataset used in the form of number of tweets and percentage. It can be seen that there is a difference in the total of number of tweets resulted from the preprocessing and labeling with slang word dictionary, which was 1952 tweets, and the one without, which was 1958 tweets.

After the dataset has been cleaned and labeled, it goes to feature extraction process. The TF-IDF feature extraction has been selected with n-gram and bigram features. The dataset was then split into two, which are the training data and the testing data. The data was then classified using Naïve Bayes and assessed to see the performance. Three combinations of ratio for data splitting, that is, 60:40, 70:30, and 80:20, were used in the experiments, and the performance evaluation results are displayed in **Figure 3**. Ratio 3 (80:20) has shown the best performance among the three as presented in **Figure 3**.

Next, main experiments were performed with the following notes:

1. The crawling data used for it was approximately 14,000 tweets crawled with the same keywords used in the preliminary works. Furthermore, the previous dataset from the preliminary work was also used in the main experiment;

2. There were four (3 + 1 self-developed) slang word dictionaries used in the main experiments, which are Okky Ibrahim (Dict. A) with 15,167 words, Louis Owen

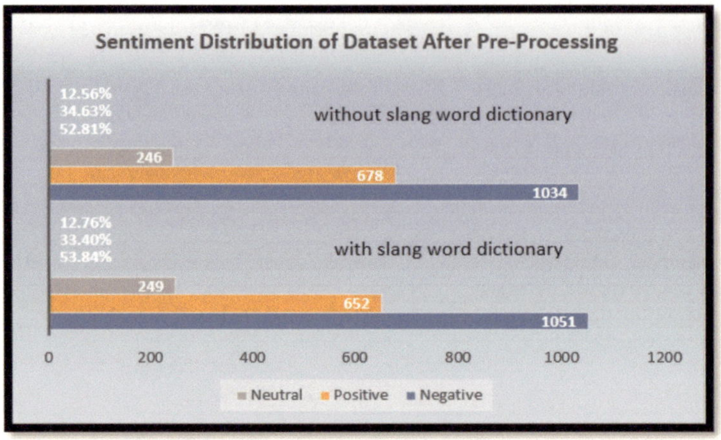

Figure 2.
Sentiment distribution of dataset after preprocessing and labeling.

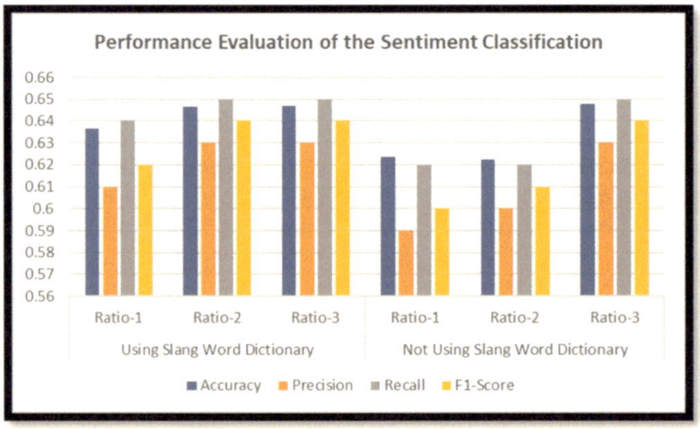

Figure 3.
Performance evaluation results of the sentiment classification process.

(Dict. B) with 1026 words, and Rama Prakoso (Dict. C) with 1319 words and our own dictionary (Dict. D) with 882 words;

3. The main experiment covered 8 different experiments as presented in **Table** 7. These main experiments were conducted at 80:20 ratio of data splitting as the results from preliminary works has shown that best performance resulted from this data splitting ratio.

Performance evaluation covering accuracy, precision, recall, and F1-score was done to each of the 16 experiments in the main phase. On top of this performance evaluation, the computation time for each experiment was observed and monitored as well. It took approximately 1 hour (59 minutes and 26 seconds) to complete conducting experiment 1 and less than 1 hour (41 minutes and 55 seconds) to conduct experiment 16. This shows that using slang word dictionary in the preprocessing of the data can reduce the total computation time required.

Experiment no.	Dictionary used	Experiment no.	Dictionary used	Experiment no.	Dictionary used
Exp. 1	No dictionary	Exp. 7	Dictionary AC	Exp. 13	Dictionary ABD
Exp. 2	Dictionary A	Exp. 8	Dictionary AD	Exp. 14	Dictionary ACD
Exp. 3	Dictionary B	Exp. 9	Dictionary BC	Exp. 15	Dictionary BCD
Exp. 4	Dictionary C	Exp. 10	Dictionary BD	Exp. 16	Dictionary ABCD
Exp. 5	Dictionary D	Exp. 11	Dictionary CD		
Exp. 6	Dictionary AB	Exp. 12	Dictionary ABC		

Table 7.
DoE of the main experiment.

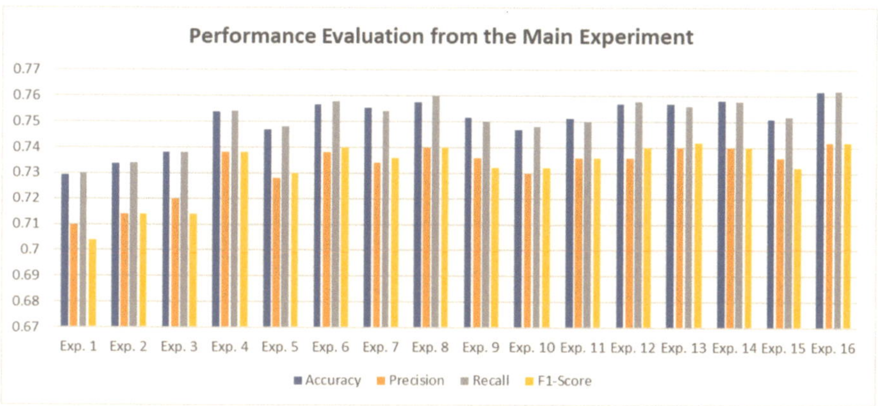

Figure 4.
Performance evaluation results from the main experiment.

The performance evaluation results in **Figure 4** show that using slang word dictionary can improve the accuracy of the sentiment classification process. Experiment 1, which did not use slang word dictionary, has the lowest accuracy compared to other experiments that used slang word dictionary. These results are also quite promising compared to another recent study conducted by [38], which reported 71.97% being the highest accuracy of the conducted sentiment analysis of tweets in social networks.

ANOVA test was then conducted to analyze whether the experimental results show significant difference between treatments [39]. Since only one factor, which is slang word dictionary, was used in the experiments, ANOVA with single factor was used for the analysis. Results from ANOVA analysis are presented in **Table 8**.

Data in **Table 8** shows that the p-value, which is $404253E^{-18}$, is way less than the significance level (0.05) of the ANOVA used. By this, it can be concluded that the null hypothesis H_0 is rejected and alternative hypothesis H_1 is accepted.

$$H_0 : \mu_1 = \mu_2 = \ldots = \mu_2 \text{ null hypothesis}$$
$$H_1 : \mu_1 \neq \mu_m \text{ alternate hypothesis.} \quad (11)$$

Source of variation	SS	df	MS	*F*	*p*-value	*F*-crit
Between groups	0.006469437	15	0.000431296	191,557,314	404253E^{-18}	182,558,574
Within groups	0.001440975	64	0.000022515			
Total	0.007910412	79				

Table 8.
The ANOVA results from the main experiment.

Where H_0: there is no significant difference in treatment of dictionary in sentiment analysis and H_1: there is a significant difference in treatment of dictionary in sentiment analysis.

In the next step, since there is a significant difference between the group of dictionaries, the least significant difference (LSD) test then can be conducted to see which group has the significant difference [40]. The test can be done by calculating it *via* the following formula. The formula was used because the same number of repetitions were performed in each experiment.

$$\mathrm{LSD} = t_{v,\alpha}\sqrt{\mathrm{MS}_{S(A)}\frac{2}{S}}$$

$$= 1.997729654\sqrt{0.0000225152352610331 * \frac{2}{5}} = 0.005995218 \qquad (12)$$

Table 9 shows the usage of the LSD as well as the notation labeling for finding the significant difference among the group of experiments.

Groups	Average	Average + LSD	Notation
Experiment 1	0.729273163	0.735268	a
Experiment 2	0.733774834	0.73977	ab
Experiment 3	0.738109573	0.744105	b
Experiment 5	0.746944543	0.75294	c
Experiment 10	0.746944543	0.75294	c
Experiment 15	0.750900742	0.756896	cd
Experiment 11	0.75132462	0.75732	cde
Experiment 9	0.751465913	0.757461	cdef
Experiment 4	0.753903214	0.759898	defg
Experiment 7	0.755351466	0.761347	defgh
Experiment 6	0.756481809	0.762477	defghi
Experiment 13	0.756870364		defghi
Experiment 12	0.756976333		efghi
Experiment 8	0.757541505		ghi
Experiment 14	0.758106676		ghi
Experiment 16	0.76156835		i

Table 9.
Results of LSD test of the main experiment.

The results in **Table 9** show that Experiment 16 is the one that has a significant difference from the other group. The concept used to determine which experiment(s) shows significant difference is based on the notation given. For example, Experiment 13 has six notations "defghi," which means that the other experiment that has the same notation does not give a significant difference toward Experiment 13. Another example is from Experiments 1 and 16; it can be seen in Experiment 1 has the notation "a," while Experiment 16 has the notation "i," which means that both experiments are significantly different from each other. Even though the last experiment, Experiment 16, bears the same notation "i" with 6, 13, 12, 8, and 14, it has the most significant difference toward the other 8 notation "a," "b," "c," "d," "e," "f," "g," and "h" and is the experiment with the highest accuracy.

In regard to the combination of dictionaries used in the research, the difference in the result of the accuracy can be seen. Experiment 1 shows 72.92% of accuracy, while Experiment 16 has 76.15% of accuracy. The amount of dictionary words used increased the accuracy of the sentiment result. However, it can be seen that the number of words from Dictionary A (Okky Ibrohim), which is 16,167 words, compared with our own dictionary that was created with the help of annotators, which only has 882 words, has raised a question. It is because when we see other groups result, for example, Experiment 12 (Dictionary ABC) with an accuracy of 75.697% and Experiment 15 (Dictionary BCD) with an accuracy of 75.090%. We further analyzed why this problem had happened, and it was because the Dictionary A was outdated with slang terms that are rarely used nowadays, although some common slang words still in use are still available there. In the dictionary D, the slang words were taken from the raw crawling data itself, taken manually and vetted by annotators, and then translated the meaning with the help of annotators as well as KBBI (Kamus Besar Bahasa Indonesia). Even though only one tenth of the Dictionary A words, there are around 270 unique words compared to the dictionary A, which help the preprocessing to be more accurate.

The above discussion shows that preprocessing with slang word dictionaries has significantly improved the performance of the sentiment analysis conducted. However, it needs to also be highlighted that the quality of the dictionary used related to its slang word collection has an effect to the contributed improvement. The research works conducted were limited to only involving four slang word dictionaries in Bahasa Indonesia, with their limited number of word collections. To determine the optimum number of slang word collections need to be used in preprocessing stage is a challenge that could significantly contribute to the sentiment analysis performance. Another limitation of this work that can be expanded further is the machine learning algorithm used. It would also be interesting to find out how the combination of different algorithm and slang word dictionary contributes to the performance of the sentiment analysis.

5. Conclusion

This study has shown that sentiment analysis can be performed well using Naïve Bayes Classifier combined with the TF-IDF for feature selection. Moreover, it also has been shown that the number of instances in the dataset used has an impact on the performance of the conducted sentiment analysis. In the preliminary stage, with the same data splitting of 80:20, the accuracy score was 64.796%, while the accuracy score in the main experiment, when the number of instances was much bigger, was 73.722% as being the lowest score. Its performance improved in about 8.926% of accuracy.

Another highlight from this study is how the inclusion of slang word dictionary in the preprocessing part has contributed to the improvement of the sentiment analysis performance. The experiment without the dictionary and all of the dictionaries combined has given different results of evaluation score, where there was improvement from 73.722% in Experiment 1 to 76.248% in Experiment 6, with an increment of 2.526% in its accuracy. In addition, the total time required for the complete sentiment analysis process has been significantly reduced, from computation time of 59 minutes and 26 seconds without slang word dictionary to 41 minutes and 55 seconds with slang word dictionary.

Author details

Media Anugerah Ayu* and Abdul Haris Muhendra
Faculty of Engineering and Technology, Sampoerna University, Jakarta, Indonesia

*Address all correspondence to: media.ayu@sampoernauniversity.ac.id

References

[1] Drus Z, Khalid H. Sentiment analysis in social media and its application: Systematic literature review. Procedia Computer Science. 2019;**161**:707-714. DOI: 10.1016/j.procs.2019.11.174

[2] Wang Y, Guo J, Yuan C, Li B. Sentiment analysis of Twitter data. Applied Sciences. 2022;**12**:11775. DOI: 10.3390/app122211775

[3] Heikal M, Torki M, El-Makky N. Sentiment analysis of Arabic tweets using deep learning. Procedia Computer Science. 2018;**142**:114-122. DOI: 10.1016/j.procs.2018.10.466

[4] Bouazizi M, Ohtsuki T. Multi-class sentiment analysis on Twitter: Classification performance and challenges. Big Data Mining and Analytics. 2019;**2**(3):181-194. DOI: 10.26599/BDMA.2019.9020002

[5] Jianqiang Z, Xiaolin G. Comparison research on text pre-processing methods on Twitter sentiment analysis. IEEE Access. 2017;**5**:2870-2879. DOI: 10.1109/access.2017.2672677

[6] Rahayu DA, Kuntur S, Hayatin N. Sarcasm detection on Indonesian twitter feeds. Proceeding of the Electrical Engineering Computer Science and Informatics. 2018;**5**(5):137-141. DOI: 10.11591/eecsi.v5i5.1724

[7] Singh T, Kumari M. Role of text pre-processing in Twitter sentiment analysis. Procedia Compuer Science. 2016;**89**: 549-554. DOI: 10.1016/j.procs.2016.06.095

[8] Maylawati DS, Zulfikar WB, Slamet C. An improved of stemming algorithm for mining Indonesian text with slang on social media. In: 6th International Conference on CYber and IT Service Management (CTTSM). 2018

[9] Yunitasari Y, Musdholifah A, Sari AK. Sarcasm detection for sentiment analysis in Indonesian tweets. Indonesian Journal of Computing and Cybernetics Systems. 2019;**13**:53-62. DOI: 10.22146/ijccs.41136

[10] Adriani M, Asian J, Nazief B, Tahaghoghi SM, Williams HE. Stemming Indonesian: A confix-stripping approach. ACM Transactions on Asian Language Information Processing. 2007;**6**(4):1-33. DOI: 10.1145/1316457.1316459

[11] Nuritha I, Arifiyanti AA, Widartha VP. Analysis of Public Perception on Organic Coffee through Text Mining Approach using Naive Bayes Classifier. In: East Indonesia Conference on Computer and Information Technology (EIConCIT). 2018. pp. 153-158. DOI: 978-1-5386-8050-6/18/$31.00

[12] Adarsh MJ, Ravikumar P. Sarcasm detection in text data to bring out genuine sentiments for sentimental analysis. In: 2019 1st International Conference on Advances in Information Technology (ICAIT). 2019. DOI: 10.1109/icait47043.2019.8987393

[13] Ferdiana R, Jatmiko F, Purwanti DD, Ayu AS, Dicka WF. Dataset Indonesia untuk Analisis Sentimen. Jurnal Nasional Teknik Elektro dan Teknologi Informasi (JNTETI). 2019;**8**(4):334-339. DOI: 10.22146/jnteti.v8i4.533

[14] Fitri VA, Andreswari R, Hasibuan MA. Sentiment analysis of social media Twitter with case of anti-LGBT campaign in Indonesia using Naïve Bayes, decision tree, and random forest algorithm. Procedia Computer Science. 2019;**161**:765-772

[15] Mandloi L, Patel R. Twitter Sentiments Analysis Using Machine Learning Methods. In: International Conference for Emerging Technology (INCET). 2020. pp. 1-5. doi:978-1-7281-6221-8/20/$31.00

[16] Casas I, Delmelle EC. Tweeting about public transit-gleaning public perceptions from a social media microblog. Case Studies on Transport Policy. 2017;**5**(4):634-642. DOI: 10.1016/j.cstp.2017.08.004

[17] Mora K, Chang J, Beatson A, Morahan C. Public perceptions of building seismic safety following the Canterbury earthquakes: A qualitative analysis using Twitter and focus groups. International Journal of Disaster Risk Reduction. 2015;**13**:1-9. DOI: 10.1016/j.ijdrr.2015.03.008

[18] Klašnja M, Barberá P, Beauchamp N, Nagler J, Tucker JA. Measuring Public Opinion with Social Media Data. In: Atkeson LR, Alvarez RM, editors. The Oxford Handbook of Polling and Survey Methods, Oxford Handbooks (2018; online ed). Oxford Academic; 5 Oct 2015. pp. 555-582. DOI: 10.1093/oxfordhb/9780190213299.013.3

[19] Al-Thubaity A, Alqahtani Q, Aljandal A. Sentiment lexicon for sentiment analysis of Saudi dialect tweets. Procedia Computer Science. 2018;**142**:301-307. DOI: 10.1016/j.procs.2018.10.494

[20] Mukhtar N, Khan MA, Chiragh N. Lexicon-based approach outperforms supervised machine learning approach for Urdu sentiment analysis in multiple domains. Telematics and Informatics. 2018;**35**(8):2173-2183. DOI: 10.1016/j.tele.2018.08.003

[21] Wu L, Morstatter F, Liu H. SlangSD: Building and using a sentiment dictionary of slang words for short-text sentiment classification. Language Resources and Evaluation. 2018;**52**(3):839-852. DOI: 10.1007/s10579-018-9416-0

[22] Salsabila NA, Winatmoko YA, Septiandri AA. Colloquial Indonesian Lexicon. In: 2018 International Conference on Asian Language Processing (IALP). 2018. pp. 226-229. DOI: 10.1109/ialp.2018.8629151

[23] Muliady W, Widiputra H. Generating Indonesian Slang Lexicons from Twitter. In: 2012 2nd International Conference on Uncertainty Reasoning and Knowledge Engineering. 2012. pp. 123-126. DOI: 10.1109/urke.2012.6319524

[24] Vieira S, Pinaya WH, Mechelli A. Introduction to machine learning. In: Mechelli A, Vieira S, editors. Machine Learning. Academic Press; 2020. pp. 1-20. DOI: 10.1016/b978-0-12-815739-8.00001-8

[25] Yeturu K. Machine learning algorithms, applications, and practices in data science. In: Srinivasa Rao ASR, Rao CR, editors. Handbook of Statistics Principles and Methods for Data Science. Elsevier; 2020. pp. 81-206. DOI: 10.1016/bs.host.2020.01.002

[26] Jianqiang Z, Xiaolin G, Xuejun Z. Deep convolution neural networks for Twitter sentiment analysis. IEEE Access. 2018;**6**:23253-23260. DOI: 10.1109/access.2017.2776930

[27] Singh S, Pareek A, Sharma A. Twitter sentiment analysis using rapid miner tool. International Journal of Computer Applications. 2019;**177**(16):44-50. DOI: 10.5120/ijca2019919604

[28] Bouazizi M, Ohtsuki T. A pattern-based approach for multi-class sentiment analysis in Twitter. IEEE Access. 2017;**5**:

20617-20639. DOI: 10.1109/access.2017.2740982

[29] Zimmer M, Proferes N. A topology of Twitter research: Disciplines, methods, and ethics. Aslib Journal of Information Management. 2014;**66**(3):250-261. DOI: 10.1108/ajim-09-2013-0083

[30] Guo X, Li J. A novel twitter sentiment analysis model with baseline correlation for financial market prediction with improved efficiency. In: Proceedings of the Sixth International Conference on Social Networks Analysis, Management and Security (SNAMS), Granada, Spain, 22–25 October 2019. 2019. pp. 472-477

[31] Harapan H, Itoh N, Yufika A, Winardi W, Keam S, Te H, et al. Coronavirus disease 2019 (COVID-19): A literature review. Journal of Infection and Public Health. 2020;**13**:667-673

[32] Kumar D, Malviya R, Sharm PK. Corona virus: A review of COVID-19. Eurasian Journal of Medicine and Oncology. 2020;**4**(10):8-25. DOI: 10.14744/ejmo.2020.51418

[33] Vieira CM, Franco OH, Restrepo CG, Abel T. COVID-19: The forgotten priorities of the pandemic. Maturitas. 2020;**136**:38-41. DOI: 10.1016/j.maturitas.2020.04.004

[34] WHO. 2019 Novel Coronavirus (2019-nCoV) Strategic Preparedness and Response Plan for the South-East Asia Region. 2020. pp. 1-22. Retrieved from World Health Organization

[35] Nicola M, Alsafi Z, Sohrabi C, Kerwan A, Al-Jabir A, Iosifidis C, et al. The socio-economic implications of the coronavirus pandemic (COVID-19): A review. International Journal of Surgery. 2020;**78**:185-193. DOI: 10.1016/j.ijsu.2020.04.018

[36] Chen L, Liu Y, Chang Y, Wang X, Luo X. Public opinion analysis of novel coronavirus from online data. Journal of Safety Science and Resilience. 2020;**1**(2):120-127. DOI: 10.1016/j.jnlssr.2020.08.002

[37] Ibrohim O, Budi I. Multi label hate speech and abusive language detection in Indonesian Twitter. ALW3: 3rd Workshop on Abusive Language Online. 2019. pp. 46-57

[38] AminiMotlagh M, Shahhoseini H, Fatehi N. A reliable sentiment analysis for classification of tweets in social networks. Social Network Analysis and Mining. 2023;**13**:7. DOI: 10.1007/s13278-022-00998-2

[39] Alassaf M, Qamar AM. Improving sentiment analysis of Arabic tweets by one-way ANOVA. Journal of King Saud University - Computer and Information Sciences. 2020;**34**(6):2849-2859. DOI: 10.1016/j. jksuci.2020.10.023

[40] Williams LJ, Abdi H. Fisher's least significant difference (LSD) test. In: Salkind N, editor. Encyclopedia of Research Design. Thousand Oaks: Sage; 2010. DOI: 10.4135/9781412961288.n154

Chapter 3

A Comparative Performance Evaluation of Algorithms for the Analysis and Recognition of Emotional Content

Konstantinos Kyritsis, Nikolaos Spatiotis, Isidoros Perikos and Michael Paraskevas

Abstract

Sentiment Analysis is highly valuable in Natural Language Processing (NLP) across domains, processing and evaluating sentiment in text for emotional understanding. This technology has diverse applications, including social media monitoring, brand management, market research, and customer feedback analysis. Sentiment Analysis identifies positive, negative, or neutral sentiments, providing insights into decision-making, customer experiences, and business strategies. With advanced machine learning models like Transformers, Sentiment Analysis achieves remarkable progress in sentiment classification. These models capture nuances, context, and variations for more accurate results. In the digital age, Sentiment Analysis is indispensable for businesses, organizations, and researchers, offering deep insights into opinions, sentiments, and trends. It impacts customer service, reputation management, brand perception, market research, and social impact analysis. In the following experimental research, we will examine the Zero-Shot technique on pre-trained Transformers and observe that, depending on the Model we use, we can achieve up to 83% in terms of the model's ability to distinguish between classes in this Sentiment Analysis problem.

Keywords: Sentiment Analysis, Natural Language Processing (NLP), sentiment classification, machine learning, transformers

1. Introduction

In this chapter, we present relatively new technologies in the field of sentiment analysis and examine their performance. The term "Sentiment Analysis" emerged and gained popularity around the late 2000s. While the concept of sentiment analysis had been present before, the term "Sentiment Analysis" was formally defined to refer to the automated processing and evaluation of sentiment expressed in texts, primarily in natural language texts. Since then, Sentiment Analysis has evolved and expanded with the development of advanced machine learning models, such as the scikit-learn library and later the Transformers. These powerful tools have significantly enhanced the capabilities of sentiment analysis by providing more accurate and efficient sentiment classification algorithms. Sentiment Analysis falls into a distinct category of text classification. It involves the process of comprehending and evaluating the sentiment expressed within a sentence, paragraph, or text. The primary objective is to identify and categorize the emotional tone conveyed in these written expressions. Sentiment Analysis commonly employs various categories to capture the nuances of sentiment. Positive category encompasses texts that convey positive emotions, including pleasure, excitement, joy, optimism, and more, Negative, where this category refers to texts that express negative emotions, such as frustration, sadness, anger, worry, and others. Finally, texts falling into Neutral category do not exhibit strong positive or negative sentiments. They often maintain an impartial stance, describing information or presenting neutral viewpoints.

It is possible to expand the aforementioned categories to five by further distinguishing between "Positive" and "Negative." This can be accomplished by introducing additional subcategories: "Very Positive" and "Positive" under the Positive category, as well as "Very Negative" and "Negative" under the Negative category. With this refinement, along with the inclusion of the Neutral category, the total number of sentiment categories becomes five. However, it is essential to exercise caution when implementing such subdivisions. Introducing more categories may have implications for evaluation metrics, as it can create ambiguity between closely related terms, making it more challenging for the model to accurately differentiate and classify them.

In general, Sentiment Analysis represents a crucial area in Natural Language Processing (NLP), offering the ability to comprehend and evaluate the emotional aspects of human expressions through automated processing. By automatically analyzing and interpreting text data, Sentiment Analysis enables us to gain insights into people's sentiments, opinions, and attitudes, thereby facilitating various applications such as market research, brand monitoring, social media analysis, and customer feedback analysis.

Transformers are a class of advanced machine learning models that have emerged in recent years and have revolutionized the field of Natural Language Processing (NLP) [1]. Unlike more traditional machine algorithms, Transformers have the ability to analyze and understand complex linguistic relationships, enabling them to solve problems like Sentiment Analysis with high levels of accuracy.

On the other hand, machine learning algorithms can also be used for Sentiment Analysis, such as Naive Bayes, Decision Trees, Random Forests, Support Vector Machines, and others. These algorithms are more traditional and rely on statistical and algebraic methods. They can be successfully applied to sentence or text-level Sentiment Analysis but may not achieve the same level of accuracy and results as Transformers.

In contrast, Transformers utilize recursive neural networks and specialized models with millions of parameters, such as BERT (Bidirectional Encoder Representations from Transformers), GPT (Generative Pre-trained Transformer), and others, which have been trained on large volumes of text data. These models can learn rich linguistic features and word compositions to recognize and categorize sentiments with high accuracy.

In summary, while the traditional Sentiment Analysis algorithms in the scikit-learn library can produce reliable results, Transformers are more advanced models capable of handling more complex linguistic problems and achieving higher accuracy in Sentiment Analysis tasks.

In the following sections, we will dive into the Zero-Shot technique, the dataset employed, the utilization of Tokenizers in Transformers, the applications of Transformers in various tasks, and a detailed examination of four pre-trained Transformer Models. We will explore how these models function and their experimental performance on the same dataset used in the Zero-Shot technique. Additionally, we will evaluate the effectiveness of each model based on various evaluation metrics and from an overall table of the models' metrics and a bar chart, we will see which model exhibits the best overall performance. The chapter will conclude with directions for future work.

2. Related works

In the literature, various works examine the use of transformers in sentiment analysis and in text classification. In the work presented in Prottasha et al. [2], the authors fine-tuned the BERT model, which had been pre-trained on the largest BanglaLM dataset. The model was subsequently combined with layers of Convolutional Neural Network (CNN) and Long Short-Term Memory (LSTM). The proposed research compared various word embedding approaches, such as Word2Vec, GloVe, fastText, and BERT. The researchers demonstrated that the transformer-based BERT model outperformed conventional techniques, achieving state-of-the-art results with sufficient fine-tuning. The study also compared several machine learning and deep learning algorithms to validate the performance of the hybrid integrated model CNN-BiLSTM (Bidirectional-LSTM). The results were analyzed using accuracy, precision, recall, F1 score, Cohen's kappa, and Receiver Operating Characteristic Area Under Curve (ROC AUC). Furthermore, the proposed model's performance was evaluated on various sentiment datasets, including the Secure Anonymised Information Linkage (SAIL) dataset, the aspect-based sentiment analysis (ABSA) dataset (cricket and restaurant parts), the BengFastText dataset, the YouTube Comments dataset, and the CogniScenti dataset. The results showed that the hybrid integrated model CNN-BiLSTM outperformed other techniques in terms of accuracy and F1 score, especially when combined with Bangla-BERT embedding.

In the work presented in Chi et al. [3], the main focus is to explore the use of pre-trained BERT models for aspect-based sentiment analysis (ABSA) tasks. The authors investigate different methods of constructing auxiliary sentences to transform ABSA into a sentence-pair classification task. These methods include question sentences, single pseudo sentences, question sentences with labels, and pseudo questions with labels. Through fine-tuning the pre-trained BERT model, they achieve new state-of-the-art results on the ABSA task using pair sentences on the datasets they evaluated. Specifically, they achieve an F1 score of 92.18 on the SentiHood dataset and an F1 score of 95.6 on the SemEval-2014 Task 4 dataset.

In the work presented in Zhang et al. [4], the authors propose a comprehensive multitask transformer network called Broad Multitask Transformer Network for Sentiment Analysis (BMT-Net) to address these issues. BMT-Net combines the strengths of feature-based and fine-tuning approaches and is specifically designed to leverage robust and contextual representations. Authors' proposed architecture ensures that the learned representations are applicable across multiple tasks through the use of multitask transformers. Furthermore, BMT-Net is capable of thoroughly learning robust contextual representations for a broad learning system, thanks to its powerful ability to explore deep and extensive feature spaces. Authors conducted experiments using two widely used datasets, namely the binary Stanford Sentiment Treebank (SST-2) and SemEval Sentiment Analysis in Twitter (Twitter). When compared to other state-of-the-art methods, authors' approach achieves superior results. Specifically, it achieves an improved F1 score of 0.778 for Twitter sentiment analysis and an accuracy of 94.0% for the SST-2 dataset. These experimental findings not only demonstrate BMT-Net's proficiency in sentiment analysis, but also emphasize the importance of previously overlooked design choices concerning the exploration of contextual features in deep and extensive domains.

In the work presented in Junyan et al. [5], the authors propose the multimodal Sparse Phased Transformer (SPT) as a solution that mitigates the complexities associated with self-attention and memory usage. SPT employs a sampling function to generate a sparse attention matrix, effectively compressing long sequences into shorter sequences of hidden states. At each layer, SPT captures interactions between hidden states from different modalities. To further enhance the efficiency of our approach, we utilize Layer-wise parameter sharing and Factorized Co-Attention. These techniques allow for parameter sharing between Cross Attention Blocks, minimizing the impact on task performance. Authors evaluate the model using three sentiment analysis datasets and achieve comparable or superior performance compared to existing methods, all the while reducing the number of parameters by 90%. Through the experiments, authors demonstrate that SPT, along with parameter sharing, can effectively capture multimodal interactions while reducing the model size and improving sample efficiency.

In the work presented in Tan et al. [6], the authors introduce a hybrid deep learning approach that combines the benefits of both sequence models and Transformer models while mitigating the limitations of sequence models. The proposed model incorporates the Robustly optimized BERT approach and Long Short-Term Memory (LSTM) for sentiment analysis. The Robustly optimized BERT approach effectively maps words into a condensed and meaningful word embedding space, while the LSTM model excels at capturing long-range contextual semantics. Through experimental evaluations, the results demonstrate that the proposed hybrid model surpasses the performance of state-of-the-art methods. It achieves impressive F1 scores of 93, 91, and 90% on the Internet Movie Database (IMDb) dataset, Twitter US Airline Sentiment dataset, and Sentiment140 dataset, respectively. These findings highlight the effectiveness of the hybrid approach in sentiment analysis tasks.

In the work presented in Tesfagergish et al. [7], authors tackle the problem of emotion detection as a component of the broader sentiment analysis task and propose a two-stage methodology. The first stage involves an unsupervised Zero-Shot learning model, which utilizes a sentence transformer to generate probabilities for 34 different emotions. This model operates without relying on labeled data. The output of the Zero-Shot model serves as input for the second stage, which involves training a supervised machine learning classifier using ensemble learning techniques and sentiment labels. Through the proposed hybrid semi-supervised approach, authors achieve the highest accuracy of 87.3% on the English SemEval 2017 dataset. This methodology effectively combines unsupervised and supervised techniques to address sentiment analysis, incorporating emotion detection and outperforming alternative methods.

3. Zero-Shot text classification

One relatively new field in research compared to other domains is Sentiment Analysis on text datasets, where models encounter classes for the first time. These transformer models are pre-trained in natural language and utilize the Zero-Shot Text Classification technique [8].

Zero-Shot Text Classification is a machine learning technique that leverages a model's ability to classify text into categories it has never seen before. This technique is applied to texts that were not used during the model's training or were not used to develop its initial understanding of the text. This means that the model can recognize and classify data (texts) into new categories that it has not "seen" during its pre-training phase. During pre-training, these models are trained on a large volume of texts from various sources, developing a general understanding of language [9].

With this technique, the models can comprehend the meaning of the text and evaluate it in relation to predefined categories provided to them, even without having seen them before. What is important here is that they recognize the meaning of these categories. As a result, these models can classify text into new categories, increasing their flexibility and applicability in various cases, such as Zero-Shot Sentiment Analysis [10].

4. Research design and methodology

4.1 Data description

In the context of our work, we explore the "Twitter US Airline Sentiment" dataset using various variations of BERT, employing the Zero-Shot text classification technique [11]. The "Twitter US Airline Sentiment" dataset is a popular collection of tweets related to US airline companies and the evaluation of their services. This dataset was published on the Kaggle platform and comprises 14,640 tweets, accompanied by comments from each customer who wrote them, the airline company mentioned in each tweet, and the corresponding sentiment category (positive, negative, or neutral). Therefore, each comment is labeled as positive, negative, or neutral. This dataset is frequently utilized in Natural Language Processing and the development of machine learning algorithms for sentiment analysis in text data. We will experimentally explore four different pre-trained Transformers using the Zero-Shot text classification technique to evaluate their performance on an unseen dataset of customer comments for airline companies. The task involves categorizing texts into positive, neutral, and negative sentiment labels, essentially performing Sentiment Analysis. These Transformers have not been previously exposed to or trained specifically on this dataset, making the evaluation more robust and insightful [11]. By investigating how these models respond to the new data, we aim to gain valuable insights into their effectiveness in sentiment analysis tasks and their adaptability to previously unseen contexts.

We will experimentally examine several pre-trained Transformer models to determine if they are effective enough to perform Sentiment classification on three classes using the Zero-Shot technique. For this purpose, we selected a dataset from Kaggle that consists of a total of 14,640 customer comments on airline companies. These comments are divided into 9781 Negative comments, 3099 Neutral comments, and 2363 Positive comments [11]. The following bar plot visually illustrates the distribution of instances based on their category. This dataset does not have a good class distribution or balance; it is imbalanced, which makes the classification task more challenging for any algorithm (Twitter US Airline Sentiment) (**Figure 1**) [12].

So, we are dealing with a quite demanding dataset for any model trained on it. However, we will examine this dataset using the Zero-Shot technique, which means without any training. Therefore, the Transformer models should have a deep understanding of the English language to achieve better results [8].

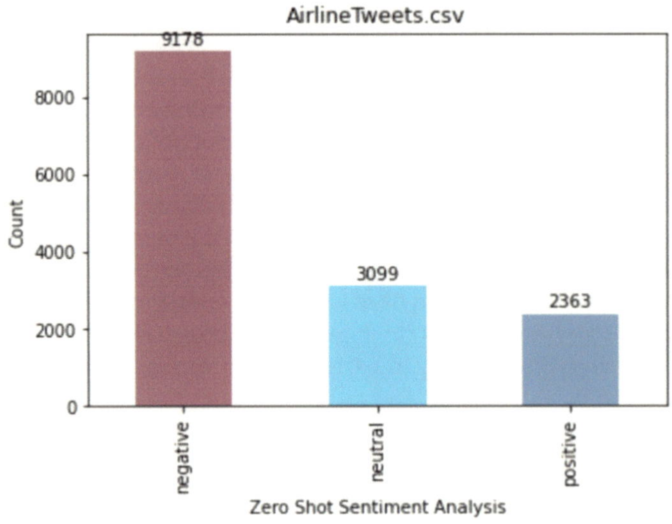

Figure 1.
Bar plot dataset's labels.

The data preprocessing, we performed, was relatively straightforward. We removed all columns that were irrelevant to our purpose, keeping only the column containing the comments and the column with the labels, which represent the actual sentiment ratings (negative, neutral, or positive). We also removed all the names of the airlines. All the other preprocessing steps that we used to do on the texts we wanted to input in the past are now handled by the built-in tokenizer of each Transformer model.

4.2 Tokenizers

4.2.1 BERT tokenizer

The BERT tokenizer is responsible for breaking down the text into smaller units called "tokens." The underlying concept of the BERT tokenizer is to represent the text using a set of tokens that correspond to significant units of the text, such as words or computational symbols.

The tokenizer operates in two main steps. First, it segments the text into words and computational symbols. Then, it converts these words and symbols into unique tokens, each of which is assigned a unique numerical identifier. This transformation allows BERT to operate with inputs of a predetermined size, as each token represents a unit of information [13].

The BERT tokenizer is designed to work in conjunction with the BERT model, creating input that represents the text by utilizing the concept of tokens. Its main function is to represent the text using a set of tokens that correspond to significant units of the text, such as words or computational symbols.

The tokenizer operates in two main steps. First, it segments the text into words and computational symbols. Then, it converts these words and symbols into unique tokens, each of which is assigned a unique numerical identifier. This transformation allows BERT to work with inputs of a fixed size, as each token represents a unit of information.

The BERT tokenizer also includes special functionalities, such as handling special characters (e.g., articles, punctuation marks) and managing the representation of words that exceed the maximum length limit by applying techniques like truncation or padding.

Using the BERT tokenizer, the input text is effectively prepared for processing by the BERT model. It enables the model to understand the meaning of the text and evaluate it in relation to pre-defined categories, without having seen them before [14].

4.2.2 DistilBERT tokenizer

The tokenizer of DistilBERT operates somewhat differently from that of BERT. DistilBERT utilizes a compressed version of BERT with fewer layers and reduced parameters. The tokenizer of DistilBERT follows a similar process as the BERT tokenizer, which involves breaking down the text into smaller units called "tokens." However, due to the reduced number of layers in DistilBERT, its tokenizer performs a simplified tokenization process. This means that the tokens of DistilBERT are fewer in comparison to BERT, and there might be a slight loss of detail in the text representation. Nevertheless, the tokenizer of DistilBERT maintains the fundamental function of the BERT tokenizer, which is to represent the text using tokens [15].

4.2.3 DistilRoBERTa tokenizer

Also, the tokenizer of DistilRoBERTa is different from that of BERT. DistilRoBERTa is based on the RoBERTa model, which is an improved version of BERT. The tokenizer of DistilRoBERTa follows a similar process to the tokenizer of BERT, where the text is broken down into smaller units called "tokens." However, there are some differences in the tokenization rules and token processing. The tokenizer of DistilRoBERTa typically uses a smaller vocabulary compared to BERT, with a limited number of tokens. This results in smaller token representations, but it can still provide high-quality performance in language tasks. Overall, the tokenizer of DistilRoBERTa is adapted to the architecture and requirements of the DistilRoBERTa model for efficiency and effective text processing.

4.3 Transformers

4.3.1 Masked language modeling (MLM)

In order to better understand Transformers and how they work in relation to Sentiment Analysis, we need to grasp one of their fundamental techniques: Masked Language Modeling (MLM).

First and foremost, it is important to know that Transformers have been designed differently depending on the task they aim to accomplish. For instance, when the task at hand is Sentiment Classification or Named Entity Recognition or Question-Answering, suitable Transformers such as BERT, DistilBERT, RoBERTa, and others have been developed specifically for these purposes. On the other hand, when our task involves translation or summarization, appropriate Transformers include Facebook's BART, Google's T5, and others. Similarly, for text generation, models like GPT, GPT2, GPT3, GPT3.5, and GPT-4 utilized by OpenAI, and others are employed.

Masked Language Modeling (MLM) is a technique used in the field of Natural Language Processing (NLP) and Machine Learning to train language models.

In Masked Language Modeling, a randomly selected word or sequence of words in a sentence is hidden (masked), and the model is tasked with predicting what that hidden word or words are. This encourages the model to understand the context and meaning of the surrounding words in order to make the prediction.

For example, a sentence that could be used in an MLM model is as follows: "The big ________ soared through the sky, capturing everyone's attention."

In this case, a word like "bird," "plane," or "kite" could be masked, and the model would need to predict the correct word within the context of the sentence.

Training MLM models is widely known, with BERT (Bidirectional Encoder Representations from Transformers) being one of the most well-known examples. BERT is trained on large bodies of text, where a random portion of words is masked, and the model attempts to predict the correct word based on the context.

Masked Language Modeling models have been successfully used in various applications, such as text completion, information retrieval, and language understanding. The idea is that MLM models can learn from the sequential content of text and reproduce human-like language understanding to a great extent. This ability adds to the model's capacity to classify or characterize texts based on sentiment [16].

4.3.2 Pre-trained models

4.3.2.1 bert-base-uncased

"bert-base-uncased" is a specific pre-trained model variant of BERT (Bidirectional Encoder Representations from Transformers). BERT is a successful machine learning model for Natural Language Processing (NLP) that is trained on large bodies of text to understand the semantic richness of words and sentence structure.

The "bert-base-uncased" version refers to a particular implementation of BERT where words are treated as lowercase (uncased), meaning they are all converted to lowercase. This means that words like "Hello" and "hello" are essentially considered the same by the model.

The difference between "bert-base-uncased" and "BERT" is that "BERT" is a general term referring to the original idea and architecture of the model, while "bert-base-uncased" is a specific implementation of that idea with specific processing parameters.

In general, the designation "bert-base-uncased" is used to describe a specific pre-trained BERT model with certain settings. There are also other variations of BERT, such as "bert-base-cased" (where uppercase and lowercase letters are preserved) and "bert-large-uncased" (a larger model size with more parameters).

As the variations of BERT can have different settings and parameters, it is important to be familiar with the descriptions and documentation to understand precisely what the differences and functionalities of each variation are [13].

4.3.2.2 distilbert-base-cased

"distilbert-base-cased" is a variation of the original BERT (Bidirectional Encoder Representations from Transformers) model that has undergone a process called "distillation" to compress the original model into a smaller size without significant loss in performance.

The differences between "distilbert-base-cased" and the original BERT lie in the following aspects:

1. Model size: "distilbert-base-cased" is significantly smaller than the original BERT. This compression is achieved by reducing the number of model layers, parameters, and nested representation layers.

2. Case sensitivity: Similar to the original BERT, "distilbert-base-cased" maintains the distinction between lowercase and uppercase letters. This means that words like "Hello" and "hello" are considered different by the model.

3. Training with knowledge distillation: The distillation process involves training the "distilbert-base-cased" model using a pre-trained BERT model as a "teacher." The smaller model attempts to replicate the performance of the original model by analyzing the knowledge transferred from the "teacher" model to the "student" model.

The main advantages of "distilbert-base-cased" are its lower memory requirements and computational power compared to the original BERT, making it suitable for applications with limited resources, such as systems with limited memory capacity or low computational power.

Overall, "distilbert-base-cased" is a compressed version of the original BERT that offers reasonably good performance relative to its size compared to the full BERT model, while requiring less space and computational power [15].

4.3.2.3 distilbert-base-uncased-mnli

"distilbert-base-uncased-mnli" is a variation of the BERT (Bidirectional Encoder Representations from Transformers) model that has been trained on the MultiNLI (Multi-Genre Natural Language Inference) dataset.

The differences of "distilbert-base-uncased-mnli" from the original BERT are as follows:

1. Model size: "distilbert-base-uncased-mnli" is compressed and smaller in size compared to the original BERT. This compression is achieved by reducing the number of layers and parameters in the model.

2. Uncased tokens: Similar to the original BERT, "distilbert-base-uncased-mnli" treats all words as uncased, disregarding the distinction between uppercase and lowercase. This means that words like "Hello" and "hello" are considered essentially the same by the model.

3. Training on the MultiNLI dataset: "distilbert-base-uncased-mnli" has been trained on the MultiNLI dataset, which includes pairs of sentences that require evaluating the relationship between them (alternative hypotheses). This trains the model to understand the logical meaning and semantics of the sentences.

Variations of BERT, such as "distilbert-base-uncased-mnli," provide pre-trained models that are adapted to specific domains and datasets. In the case of "distilbert-base-uncased-mnli," it has been specifically trained on the MultiNLI dataset for better performance in logical analysis and evaluating the relationship between sentences.

Overall, "distilbert-base-uncased-mnli" is a compressed variation of the BERT model that has been trained on the MultiNLI dataset. This variation offers a smaller model size while maintaining the ability to comprehend and evaluate the relationship between sentences [15].

4.3.2.3.1 MultiNLI (multi-genre natural language inference)

The MultiNLI (Multi-Genre Natural Language Inference) dataset is a popular dataset used in the field of Natural Language Processing (NLP) to evaluate the ability of models to understand the meaning and relationship between sentences.

The MultiNLI dataset consists of pairs of sentences known as "hypothesis" and "premise." The "hypothesis" is a statement expressing an idea or hypothesis, while the "premise" is the sentence from which the hypothesis is derived. The main task is to evaluate whether the hypothesis is "entailment," "contradiction," or "neutral" based on the relationship between the two sentences.

MultiNLI encompasses a variety of linguistic materials, covering different genres of literature, scientific texts, news articles, and other types of written material. This ensures the diversity and generalization of the dataset, ensuring that models trained on it can comprehend and respond to various linguistic scenarios.

MultiNLI has been widely used as a dataset for evaluating and training NLP models, including BERT models. Using MultiNLI, we can study a model's ability to understand the meaning of sentences and process the relationships between them.

Overall, MultiNLI represents an important dataset for the development and evaluation of NLP models that deal with recognizing and evaluating the relationship between sentences [17].

4.3.2.4 nli-distilroberta-base

Let us first examine RoBERTa in relation to BERT to understand the version of the pre-trained model nli-distilroberta-base:

RoBERTa is a pre-trained model for Natural Language Processing (NLP) that is a variation of the original BERT (Bidirectional Encoder Representations from Transformers) model. The name "RoBERTa" stands for "Robustly Optimized BERT approach."

The differences between RoBERTa and the original BERT are as follows:

1. Text preprocessing: During text preprocessing, RoBERTa eliminates the case distinction between uppercase and lowercase letters. This means that all letters are converted to lowercase before being processed by the model. This approach allows the model to treat words with different cases as completely different.

2. More training data: RoBERTa is trained on a larger dataset compared to the original BERT. Instead of using 16% of the BERT dataset, RoBERTa utilizes the full datasets of BooksCorpus (800 million words) and CC-News (CommonCrawl News) (76 gigabytes).

3. Training duration: The training algorithm of RoBERTa takes longer than the algorithm used for the original BERT. This means that RoBERTa is trained for more epochs and for a longer period of time to better leverage the available data and improve its performance. These differences constitute enhancements that allow RoBERTa to achieve better results in various NLP tasks compared to the original BERT. However, it is important to note that the fundamental

architecture and ideas that guided BERT remain at the core of RoBERTa, with the differences mainly focusing on training and data preprocessing.

4. Larger model size: RoBERTa has a larger model size compared to the original BERT. This implies that RoBERTa has more parameters and a more detailed representation of words and sentences [18].

The above differences constitute improvements that allow RoBERTa to achieve better results in various NLP tasks compared to the original BERT. However, it is important to note that the basic architecture and ideas that guided BERT remain at the core of RoBERTa, with the differences focusing on training and data preprocessing [18].

Therefore, "nli-distilroberta-base" is a pre-trained model for Natural Language Processing (NLP) that is a variation of the original BERT (Bidirectional Encoder Representations from Transformers) model. This variation utilizes the DistilRoBERTa architecture and has been trained on the NLI (Natural Language Inference) dataset.

The differences of "nli-distilroberta-base" from the original BERT are as follows:

1. Architecture: "nli-distilroberta-base" utilizes the DistilRoBERTa architecture, which is a simplified version of the RoBERTa model. The DistilRoBERTa architecture uses fewer layers and parameters compared to the original BERT, aiming to reduce the size of the model.

2. Training on the NLI dataset: "nli-distilroberta-base" has been trained on the NLI dataset, which consists of sentence pairs for evaluating the relationship between them. Training on the NLI dataset helps the model understand the meaning and relationship between different sentences [11].

5. Experimental results

We will describe the results we obtained from the experimental process of four pre-trained Transformers on the same dataset (Twitter US Airline Sentiment) that we described earlier [12]. The experiments were conducted by us using our own computational resources. The code for the metrics we present was written in Python, utilizing relevant libraries for Transformers with pipelines for the Zero-Shot technique. All Confusion Matrices were generated by combining two functions: confusion_matrix from the sklearn.metrics library and sns.heatmap from the seaborn library.

5.1 Zero-Shot and sentiment analysis distilbert-base-cased

Applying the Zero-Shot technique to the pre-trained Transformer distilbert-base-cased, we obtain the Confusion Matrix (**Figure 2**).

The diagonal of the Confusion Matrix always shows the percentages that the Transformer predicted correctly (**Table 1**). So here we can see that the Transformer correctly predicted 18% of the positive sentiments, 25% of the negative sentiments, and 60% of the neutral sentiments. In the other cells, we can observe the following:

- 23% of the comments that were actually positive were predicted as negative by the model.

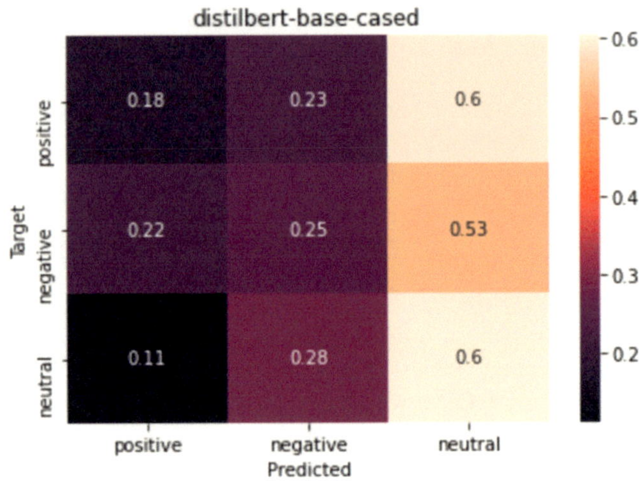

Figure 2.
Confusion Matrix of distilbert-base-cased.

distilbert-base-cased (3 classes)		
Val_accuracy	**f1_score**	**roc_auc_score**
31.14×10^{-2}	31.14×10^{-2}	53.11×10^{-2}

Table 1.
Metrics of distilbert-base-cased.

- 60% of the comments that were actually positive were predicted as neutral by the model.
- 22% of the comments that were actually negative were predicted as positive by the model.
- 53% of the comments that were actually negative were predicted as neutral by the model.
- 11% of the comments that were actually neutral were predicted as positive by the model.
- 28% of the comments that were actually neutral were predicted as negative by the model.
- Val_accuracy = 0.3114071038251366: This metric represents the percentage of correct predictions overall, and we can see that it is approximately 31.14%.
- F1_score = 0.3114071038251366: The F1 score combines precision and recall and measures the balance between them. In your case, the F1 score is also approximately 31.14%.
- Roc_auc_score = 0.531066885655905: The ROC AUC score (Receiver Operating Characteristic Area Under Curve) measures the model's ability to distinguish

between classes. A score of 0.5 represents randomness, while a score of 1 represents perfect discrimination. In your case, the ROC AUC score is approximately 0.531, suggesting a moderate ability to discriminate between classes.

Overall, the model appears to have relatively low performance based on the presented metrics. This could be because the pre-trained model may not have adequately understood such comments, which often contain irony or sarcasm. This does not mean that pre-trained Transformers cannot understand such comments; it means that this specific model has not reached the levels of language comprehension required for use in Zero-Shot Sentiment Classification.

5.2 Zero-Shot and sentiment analysis bert-base-uncased

Applying the Zero-Shot technique to the pre-trained Transformer bert-base-uncased, we obtain the Confusion Matrix (**Figure 3**).

The diagonal of the Confusion Matrix always shows the percentages that the Transformer predicted correctly. So here we can see that the Transformer correctly predicted 58% of the negative sentiments, 17% of the neutral sentiments, and 40% of the positive sentiments. In the other cells, we can observe the following (**Table 2**).

- 16% of the comments that were actually negative were predicted as neutral by the model.
- 26% of the comments that were actually negative were predicted as positive by the model.
- 46% of the comments that were actually neutral were predicted as negative by the model.
- 36% of the comments that were actually neutral were predicted as positive by the model.

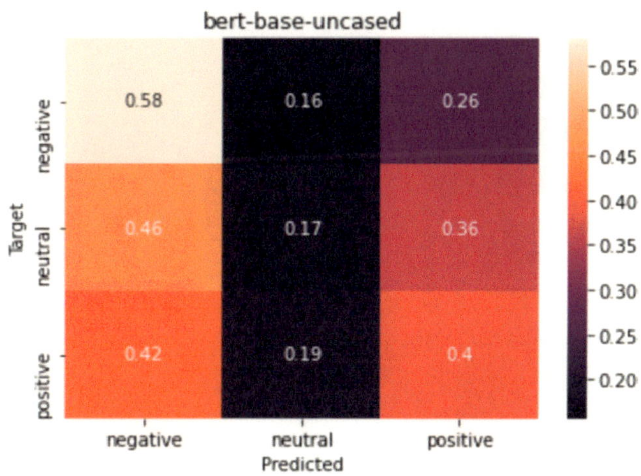

Figure 3.
Confusion Matrix of bert-base-uncased.

bert-base-uncased (3 classes)		
Val_accuracy	**f1_score**	**roc_auc_score**
46.45×10^{-2}	46.45×10^{-2}	50.83×10^{-2}

Table 2.
Metrics of bert-base-uncased.

- 42% of the comments that were actually positive were predicted as negative by the model.
- 19% of the comments that were actually positive were predicted as neutral by the model.

Based on the metrics provided for the Transformer bert-base-uncased for sentiment analysis with Zero-Shot text classification, we can draw the following conclusions:

The validation accuracy is low, at 0.4644808743169399. This indicates that the model struggles in recognizing the three classes in the dataset.

The F1 score for the model is 0.4644808743169399, representing the harmonic mean of precision and recall. This suggests that the model has limited performance in both precision and recall.

The ROC AUC score is 0.5083023131851064, which is low. This indicates that the model has limited ability to correctly distinguish the three classes.

5.3 Zero-Shot and sentiment analysis distilbert-base-uncased-mnli

Applying the Zero-Shot technique to the pre-trained Transformer distilbert-base-uncased-mnli, we obtain the Confusion Matrix (**Figure 4**).

The diagonal of the Confusion Matrix always shows the percentages that the Transformer predicted correctly. So here we can see that the Transformer correctly

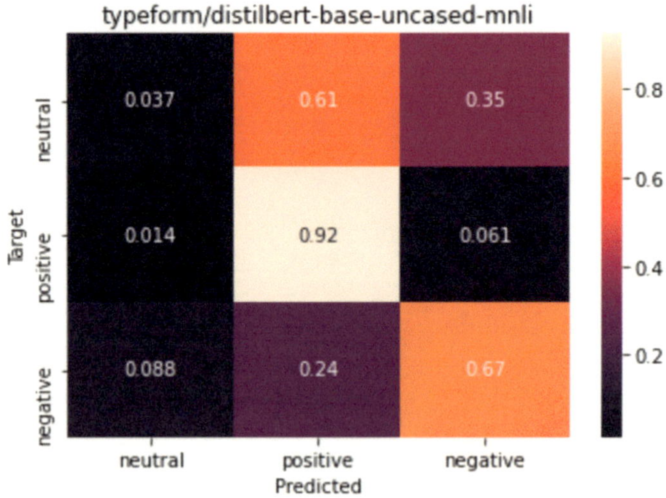

Figure 4.
Confusion Matrix of distilbert-base-uncased-mnli.

typeform/distilbert-base-uncased-mnli (3 classes)		
Val_accuracy	**f1_score**	**roc_auc_score**
57.61×10^{-2}	57.61×10^{-2}	76.83×10^{-2}

Table 3.
Metrics of distilbert-base-uncased-mnli.

predicted 3.7% of the neutral sentiments, 92% of the positive sentiments, and 67% of the negative sentiments. In the other cells, we can observe the following (**Table 3**).

- 61% of the comments that were actually neutral were predicted as positive by the model.
- 35% of the comments that were actually neutral were predicted as negative by the model.
- 1.4% of the comments that were actually positive were predicted as neutral by the model.
- 6.1% of the comments that were actually positive were predicted as negative by the model.
- 8.8% of the comments that were actually negative were predicted as neutral by the model.
- 24% of the comments that were actually negative were predicted as positive by the model.

Based on the metrics provided for the Transformer distilbert-base-uncased-mnli for sentiment analysis with Zero-Shot text classification, we can draw the following conclusions:

Validation accuracy (Val_accuracy): The validation accuracy is 0.576. This means that the Transformer correctly classifies the sentiment of the text into three categories (3 classes) with an average accuracy of 57.6%. This accuracy indicates that the Transformer has a relatively moderate performance, and there is room for improvement.

F1 score: The F1 score is 0.576, which is equal to the validation accuracy. The F1 score is a measure of the overall performance that combines precision and recall. The value of 0.576 indicates that the Transformer has a moderate performance and needs improvement in this area.

ROC AUC score: The ROC AUC score is 0.768. This metric evaluates the model's ability to distinguish between classes and correctly rank examples based on the predicted probabilities. A ROC AUC score of 0.768 indicates that the Transformer has a relatively good discriminative ability between classes, but there is still room for improvement.

Overall, we can say that the Transformer distilbert-base-uncased-mnli has a moderate performance in sentiment analysis with Zero-Shot text classification, and there is room for improvement in terms of accuracy and F1 score. However, the ability to distinguish between classes, as represented by the ROC AUC score, is relatively good.

5.4 Zero-Shot and sentiment analysis nli-distilroberta-base

Applying the Zero-Shot technique to the pre-trained Transformer nli-distilroberta-base, we obtain the Confusion Matrix (**Figure 5**).

The diagonal of the Confusion Matrix always shows the percentages that the Transformer predicted correctly. So here we can see that the Transformer correctly predicted 4.4% of the neutral sentiments, 87% of the positive sentiments, and 86% of the negative sentiments. In the other cells, we can observe the following (**Table 4**).

- 39% of the comments that were actually neutral were predicted as positive by the model.
- 57% of the comments that were actually neutral were predicted as negative by the model.
- 2.0% of the comments that were actually positive were predicted as neutral by the model.
- 11% of the comments that were actually positive were predicted as negative by the model.
- 3.3% of the comments that were actually negative were predicted as neutral by the model.

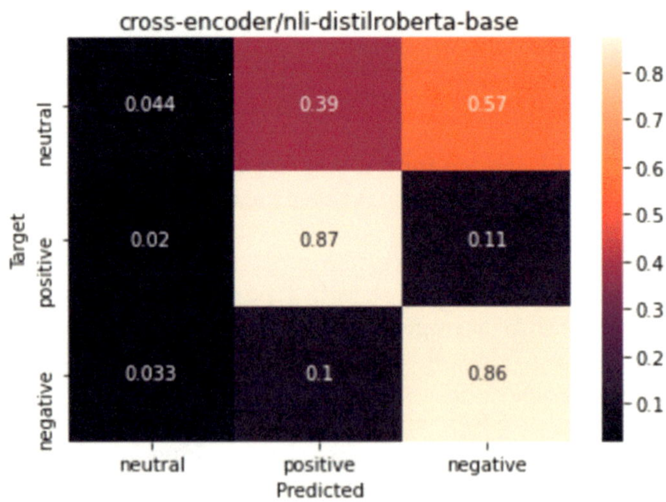

Figure 5.
Confusion Matrix of nli-distilroberta-base.

cross-encoder/nli-distilroberta-base (3 classes)		
Val_accuracy	**f1_score**	**roc_auc_score**
69.17×10^{-2}	69.17×10^{-2}	82.63×10^{-2}

Table 4.
Metrics of nli-distilroberta-base.

- 10% of the comments that were actually negative were predicted as positive by the model.

Based on the metrics provided for the Transformer nli-distilroberta-base, which performs sentiment analysis using Zero-Shot text classification, we can draw the following conclusions:

1. Validation accuracy (Val_accuracy): The validation accuracy is 0.692. This indicates that the Transformer correctly classifies the sentiment of the text into three categories (3 classes) with an accuracy of 69.2%. This accuracy shows a relatively good performance, suggesting that the Transformer is effective in predicting sentiment.

2. F1 score: The F1 score is 0.692, which is equal to the validation accuracy. The F1 score combines precision and recall and provides an overall measure of performance. The value of 0.692 indicates that the Transformer has a relatively good balance between precision and recall, resulting in accurate predictions for sentiment analysis.

3. ROC AUC score: The ROC AUC score is 0.826. This metric evaluates the model's ability to differentiate between classes and rank examples based on predicted probabilities. A ROC AUC score of 0.826 indicates that the Transformer has a good discriminative ability, with a high likelihood of correctly distinguishing between different sentiment classes.

In summary, the Transformer nli-distilroberta-base demonstrates a relatively good performance in sentiment analysis using Zero-Shot text classification. It achieves high accuracy, F1 score, and ROC AUC score, indicating its effectiveness in accurately predicting sentiment and distinguishing between different sentiment classes (**Table 5** and **Figure 6**).

Based on the overall table for the performances of the Transformers we have and the bar plot, we can draw the following conclusions:

Validation accuracy: The models significantly differ in validation accuracy. The nli-distilroberta-base model has the highest validation accuracy at around 69.2%, while the distilbert-base-cased model has the lowest validation accuracy at around 31.1%.

F1 score: Similar to the validation accuracy, the nli-distilroberta-base model achieves the highest F1 score at around 69.2%, while the distilbert-base-cased model has the lowest F1 score at around 31.1%.

ROC AUC score: The nli-distilroberta-base model has the highest ROC AUC score at around 82.6%, indicating a good discriminative ability between classes.

Transformers	Validation accuracy	F1 score	ROC AUC score
distilbert-base-cased	31.14×10^{-2}	31.14×10^{-2}	53.11×10^{-2}
bert-base-uncased	46.45×10^{-2}	46.45×10^{-2}	50.83×10^{-2}
distilbert-base-uncased-mnli	57.61×10^{-2}	57.61×10^{-2}	76.83×10^{-2}
nli-distilroberta-base	69.17×10^{-2}	69.17×10^{-2}	82.63×10^{-2}

Table 5.
Comparison in the metrics of all models.

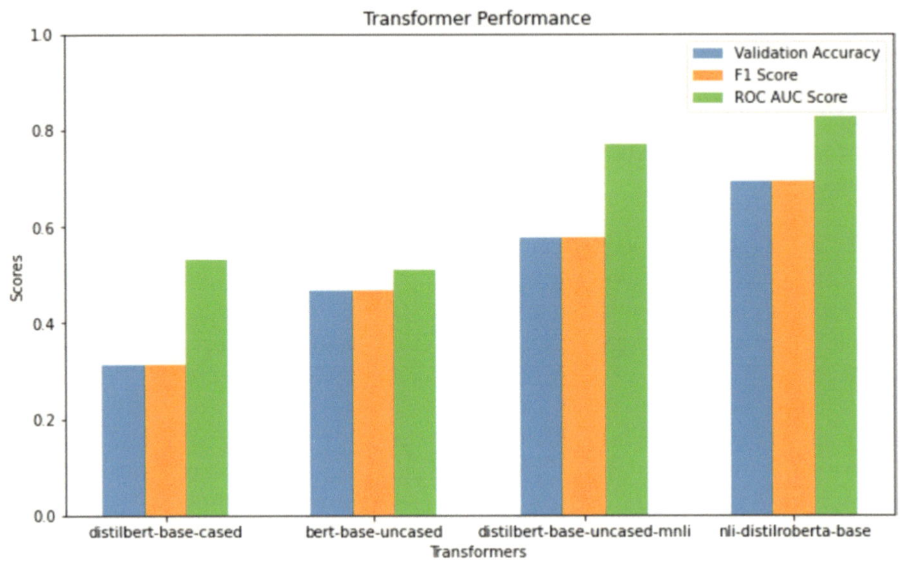

Figure 6.
Bar plot comparison of all models.

On the contrary, the distilbert-base-cased model has the lowest ROC AUC score at around 53.1%.

Overall, the nli-distilroberta-base model stands out among the other three models in all metrics. It demonstrates higher validation accuracy, F1 score, and ROC AUC score compared to the other models. On the other hand, the distilbert-base-cased model shows the lowest performance across all metrics.

Therefore, we can conclude that the nli-distilroberta-base model is the most effective among the four models examined for sentiment analysis.

6. Conclusions

The fact that we followed the Zero-Shot Sentiment Classification technique limits us in terms of fine-tuning to achieve optimal results in Sentiment Analysis for this specific dataset. Through these experiments, a new technique is highlighted, which can be applied to vast datasets. With the Zero-Shot technique, we can achieve Sentiment Classification without human supervision. One might wonder how many human hours are required to evaluate a massive dataset without errors. This method can be likened to unsupervised learning. Furthermore, it is another approach to understand how well the pre-trained Model has immersed itself in the language.

The percentages we achieved in the experiments demonstrate to what extent this particular Transformer Model has been trained on similar data and how well it has understood the language. Such an effort to apply the Zero-Shot Sentiment Classification technique on the Twitter US Airline Sentiment dataset has not been done before, so there is no comparative reference we can provide. However, works have been done with this technique in other domains, such as a study proposing a method for conducting Zero-Shot Aspect-Based Sentiment Analysis without using domain-specific training data, among others [19].

The abundance of user-generated information on the Web necessitates accurate methods for analyzing and determining users' opinions and attitudes toward events, products, and entities. In this study, we designed and implemented BERT-like Transformers for the task of Zero-Shot classification. These four pre-trained Transformer models deliver commendable results, despite having only a few million parameters.

Future work will focus on several directions based on the presented results in this chapter using the Zero-Shot technique. First, exploring other models known for their performance in sentiment analysis with the Zero-Shot technique should be considered. Evaluating their accuracy, F1 score, and ROC AUC score and comparing them to those of the existing models will be beneficial. Experimenting with different model variations to identify the most suitable one for specific requirements is recommended. Additionally, examining data preprocessing techniques and evaluating the steps involved in data preprocessing should be conducted. Lastly, exploring ensemble models that combine multiple models to enhance performance can be advantageous. The utilization of diverse models can offer improvements in terms of accuracy and overall performance. These are potential avenues for future work to enhance the results of sentiment analysis using the Zero-Shot techniques.

Acknowledgements

We would like to express our gratitude to Mr. Panagiotis Hadjidoukas from the Department of Computer Logic, part of the Department of Computer Engineering & Informatics at the University of Patras, for providing us with the computational resources necessary to conduct these demanding experiments.

This work was partially supported by the Project entitled "Strengthening the Research Activities of the Directorate of Infrastructure and Networks," funded by the Computer Technology Institute and Press "Diophantus" with project code 0822/001.

Author details

Konstantinos Kyritsis[1,2], Nikolaos Spatiotis[1,2], Isidoros Perikos[1,2,3] and Michael Paraskevas[1,2]*

1 Computer Technology Institute and Press "Diophantus," Patras, Greece

2 Electrical and Computer Engineering Department, University of Peloponnese, Greece

3 Computer Engineering and Informatics Department, University of Patras, Greece

*Address all correspondence to: mparask@cti.gr

References

[1] Vaswani A, Shazeer N, Parmar N, Uszkoreit J, Jones L, Gomez AN, et al. Attention Is All You Need. New York: Cornell University Library in Ithaca; 2017. Available from: https://arxiv.org/abs/1706.03762

[2] Prottasha NJ, Sami AA, Kowsher M, Murad SA, Bairagi AK, Masud M, et al. Transfer learning for sentiment analysis using BERT based supervised fine-tuning. Sensors. 2022;**22**(11):4157

[3] Chi S, Luyao H, Xipeng Q. Utilizing BERT for aspect-based sentiment analysis. arxiv.org. In: Proceedings of the 2019 Conference of the North American Chapter of the Association for Computational Linguistics: Human Language Technologies, vol. 1; 2019. pp. 380-385. Available from: https://aclanthology.org/N19-1035/

[4] Zhang T, Gong X, Chen CLP. BMT-net: Broad multitask transformer network for sentiment analysis. IEEE Access. 2022;**52**(7):6232-6243. Available from: https://ieeexplore.ieee.org/document/9369997

[5] Cheng J, Fostiropoulos I, Boehm B, Soleymani M. Multimodal phased transformer for sentiment analysis. In: Conference on Empirical Methods in Natural Language Processing. United States: Association for Computational Linguistics (ACL); 2021. Available from: https://aclanthology.org/2021.emnlp-main.189/

[6] Tan KL, Lee CP, Lim KM, Anbananthen KSM. Sentiment analysis with ensemble hybrid deep. IEEE Access. 2022;**10**:103694-103704. Available from: https://doaj.org/article/948b7ca90291416fb31bda6b789b8920

[7] Tesfagergish SG, Kapočiūtė-Dzikienė J, Damaševičius R. Zero-Shot emotion detection for semi-supervised sentiment analysis using sentence transformers and ensemble learning. Applied Sciences. 2022;**12**(17):8662

[8] Yang P, Wang J, Gan R, Zhu X, Zhang L, Wu Z, et al. Zero-Shot learners for natural language understanding via a unified multiple choice perspective. In: Proceedings of the 2022 Conference on Empirical Methods in Natural Language Processing. Pennsylvania, United States: Association for Computational Linguistics (ACL); 2022

[9] Yin W, Hay J and Roth D. Benchmarking Zero-Shot text classification: Datasets, evaluation and entailment approach. In: IJCNLP 2019. Pennsylvania, United States: Association for Computational Linguistics (ACL); 2019. Available from: https://aclanthology.org/D19-1404/

[10] Pushp PK, Srivastava MM. Train once, test anywhere: Zero-Shot learning for text classification. arXiv: Computation and Language. 2017. [preprint]

[11] Delangue C, Chaumond J, Wolf T. Hugging Face [Online]. U.S.: Hugging Face, Inc.; 2016. Available from: https://huggingface.co/

[12] Sculley D, Elliott J, Hamner B, Moser J. Kaggle [Online]. 2010. Available from: https://www.kaggle.com/crowdflower/twitter-airline-sentiment

[13] Devlin J, Ming-Wei C, Kenton L and Kristina T. BERT: Pre-training of deep bidirectional transformers for language understanding. United States: Association for Computational

Linguistics (ACL); 2019. DOI: 10.48550/arXiv.1810.04805.

[14] Kudo T, Richardson J. SentencePiece: A simple and language independent subword tokenizer and detokenizer for neural text processing. In: Empirical Methods in Natural Language Processing: System Demonstrations. Pennsylvania, United States: Association for Computational Linguistics (ACL); 2018

[15] Sanh V, Debut L, Chaumond J, Wolf T. DistilBERT, a distilled version of BERT: Smaller, faster, cheaper and lighter. In: 5th Workshop on Energy Efficient Machine Learning and Cognitive Computing-NeurIPS 2019. Vancouver; 2020

[16] Salazar J, Liang D, Nguyen TQ, Kirchhoff K. Masked language model scoring. In: Proceedings of the 58th Annual Meeting of the Association for Computational Linguistics [Online]. Pennsylvania, United States: Association for Computational Linguistics (ACL); 2020. Available from: https://aclanthology.org/2020.acl-main.240/

[17] Raffel C, Shazeer N, Roberts A, Lee K, Narang S, Matena M, et al. Exploring the limits of transfer learning with a unified text-to-text transformer. Journal of Machine Learning Research. 2020;**21**:1-67

[18] Liu Y, Ott M, Goyal N, Du J, Joshi M, Chen D, et al. RoBERTa: A robustly optimized BERT Pretraining approach. In: Proceedings of the 20th Chinese National Conference on Computational Linguistics. Huhhot; 2021

[19] Shu L, Xu H, Liu B, Chen J. Zero-Shot Aspect-Based Sentiment Analysis. 2022. Available from: https://arxiv.org/pdf/2202.01924.pdf

Section 3

Future Roadmap

Chapter 4

Sentiment Analysis of Social Media Using Artificial Intelligence

K. Victor Rajan

Abstract

Social media refers to the development and sharing of sentiment, information, and interests, as well as other forms of opinion via virtual communities and networks. Nowadays, social networking and micro blogging websites are considered reliable sources of information since users may openly express their opinions in these forums. An investigation of the sentiment on social media could assist decision-makers in learning how consumers feel about their services, products, or policies. Extracting emotion from social media messages is a difficult task due to the difficulty of Natural Language Processing (NLP). These messages frequently use a combination of graphics, emoticons, text, etc. to convey the sentiment or opinion of the general people. These claims, known as eWOM (Electronic Word of Mouth), are quite common in public forums where people may express their opinions. A classification issue arises when categorizing the sentiment of eWOM as positive, negative, or neutral. We could not use standard NLP tools to examine social media sentiment. In this chapter, we will study the role of Artificial Intelligence in identifying the sentiment polarity of social media. We will apply ML(Machine Learning) methods to resolve this classification issue without diving into the difficulty of eWOM parsing.

Keywords: social media analytics, sentiment analysis, artificial intelligence, electronic word of mouth, machine learning

1. Introduction

Sentiment polarity has a context-sensitive meaning in sentiment analysis. Based on the sum of the positive and negative opinions stated about an event, automatic methods calculate the sentiment polarity. Generally, daily sentiment scores are often calculated by measuring the number of positive as well as negative words in a sentence. A sentence with more negative words (reflecting violence, anger, sadness) than positive (displaying happiness, celebration, joy) is deemed negative.

Definition: Sentiment polarity of textual data is the result of analysis expressed in terms of a numerical value obtained by the algebraic sum of opinion contained in each entity of the sentence, document, or message. The sentiment polarity can be determined as positive, negative, or neutral.

Sentiment polarity score (S_p) of a message is the linear combination of all polarities. This is in turn converted as a ratio to the sum to get a rational value between -1 and 1. Hence,

$$S_p = (W_p\text{-}\ W_n)/(W_p + W_n) \quad (1)$$

where W_p denotes the number of positive words in the and W_n represents a number of negative words in the message.

Several decision-makers, including business organizations and governmental authorities, may learn more about public opinion by using social media analytics. Short messages are used by users to share their opinions on social networking platforms. Sentiment analysis of social media evaluates emotions and opinions [1]. These social media messages reflecting the opinion, sentiment, and emotion of the public via a combination of text, images, and emoticons are sometimes referred to as eWOM.

Definition: eWOM refers to messages that are written to be exposed via internet-mediated online communication, especially towards a brand, product, or organization.

The field of social media analysis has grown up fast in this decade to answer the question 'What do people feel about a certain event or topic?'. Analyzing the sentiments, opinions, and emotions of people has its importance. For instance, we could assess a community's well-being; we can stop suicides, etc. Additionally, by examining client feedback, businesses may gain a great deal of insight into the level of consumer satisfaction. However, the non-standard format of these messages makes it challenging to understand the language of eWOM. For example, the message 'Enjoying my lazy Sunday 😊!!' is a mix of words and emoji representing positive sentiment about Sunday. An eWOM like this is difficult for parsing because it contains special and emoticons symbols. The context of the sentence could not be interpreted unless parsers are also familiar with the meaning of the emoji 😊. Sentiment analysis would not be correct until these messages are translated into plain text while retaining their context and emotions.

Social media users always express their sentiments over a product or a public event. A user-generated message containing sentiment can be defined as a quadruple:

$$\mathrm{u} = (\mathrm{o}, \mathrm{f}, \mathrm{s}, \mathrm{h}) \quad (2)$$

here
o indicates a target object.
f represents a feature of the object.
s denotes the sentiment value of the opinion (+ve, −ve, or neutral).
h signifies opinion holder.
For example, the following is a user review of mobile phones.

Although the battery life of my new phone is not long, that is ok for me.

When we parse this message, we get the quadruple as follows:
o new phone.
f battery life.
s not long (-ve sentiment).
h ok for me.

Sentiment analysis involves major sub-tasks namely pre-processing, transformation, and classification. Though pre-processing and transformation can be done using text manipulation, classification is a complex task. It involves recognizing the sentiment along with the context. The system should interpret the meaning and analyze the sentiment similar to human intelligence. A systematic methodology is needed as shown below.

- Cleansing and extracting textual content from eWOM.
- Identifying the sentiment polarity of the extracted text.

Artificial Intelligence (AI) is a powerful source for the crowd's wisdom to filter out non-textual information and our study focuses on how artificial intelligence can effectively be used to identify the sentiment of eWOM.

2. Architecture of social sentiment analysis system

After extracting plain text from social media messages, we can use computer algorithms to automatically classify the sentiment polarity. The following two categories might be used to broadly classify sentiment analysis algorithms:

i. **Lexicon based**: This method uses a pre-built repository of emotional words to match the message. A knowledge base having textual units annotated with sentiment labels is called an emotion lexicon. They depend on lexical resources such as lexicon, word banks, or ontology.

ii. **AI-based**: AI-based approaches use ML methods to identify the sentiment. The machine learning approach uses algorithms that may learn from data by making use of document similarity between text messages.

The subjectivity, polarity, or object of any opinion is frequently determined by a lexicon-based system using a set of criteria created by people. These rules may take into account a variety of NLP methods developed in computational linguistics, like part-of-speech tagging, tokenization, stemming, and parsing.

Contrary to lexicon-based systems, AI-based methods are on the basis of ML algorithms instead of hand-crafted rules. Typically, the process of identifying the polarity of sentiment is defined as a classification problem, in which a classifier is provided a text and outputs a polarity label, like positive, negative, or neutral.

Lexicon-based systems do not perform well due to the non-standard language of social media users. Results are more accurate, which is one major advantage of AI-based systems. They resemble a human scoring system while classifying the sentiment polarity by taking the contextual information into account. Machine Learning algorithms are widely used to solve complex real-world problems. It is a promising strategy that has been widely used in AI disciplines including NLP, semantic parsing, transfer learning, computer vision, and many others. Social media sentiment analysis is a complicated task because of the following difficulties:

- People do not have a formal writing style.
- People use colloquial and personal elements in their language.

- People use a mixture of text, emojis, abbreviations, images, and symbols.
- Hashtags are also often used to highlight their importance.
- Millions of messages are generated every second.

Automatic systems try to extract the sentiment polarity using computer algorithms and techniques. The colloquial language makes it hard for automatic systems to interpret the context and sentiment being expressed. The sentiment analysis methodology we show here employs machine learning methods to classify sentiment at the sentence level and acts directly at that level (**Figure 1**).

The first step is to translate the eWOM into plain English text using pre-defined mapping for symbols and emojis. The text is then converted to a feature vector representing the features. The Ml method creates a model from pairs of feature vectors and labels (such as positive and negative), which are input into the process. The well-trained model predicts sentiment polarity for new incoming input.

3. Feature engineering of messages

Social media messages are not well-formed and unstructured. The system for analyzing sentiment needs to be tailored to handle the style and specifics of this informal writing style. For example, the message "Enjoying my lazy Sunday 😊" signifies a positive sentiment. It comprises one word and one emoji representing happiness. Feature engineering is the method of selecting and transforming unprocessed data into features that could be utilized in ML. The inclusion of symbols and emojis plays a significant role in detecting hidden sentiments. The first step in processing the eWOM is feature engineering. We need to derive meaningful sentences

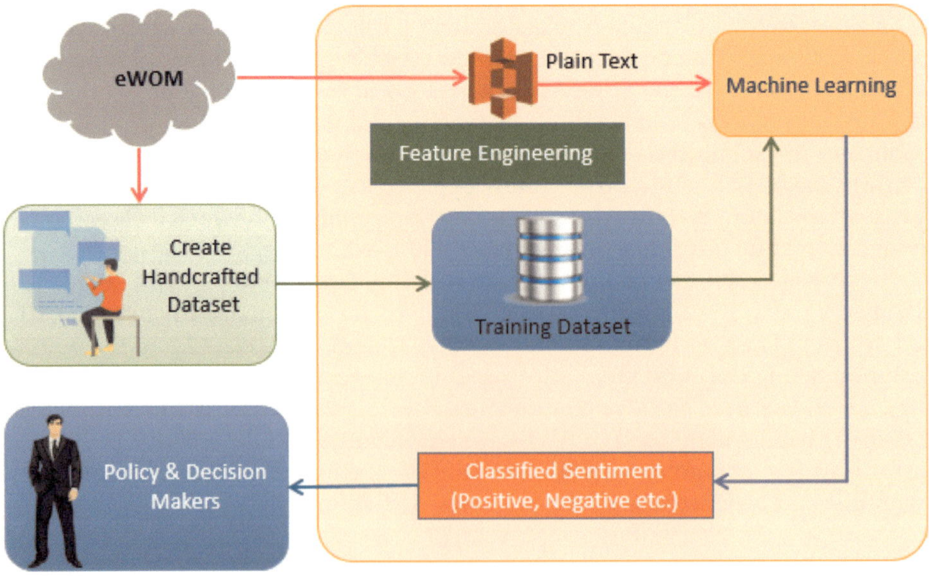

Figure 1.
Architecture of sentiment analysis system.

from eWOM so that the message is informative, non-redundant and supports the next learning and generalization steps [2]. Feature engineering (FE) works as follows.

- Emojis are replaced with Common Locale Data Repository meaning if a mapping is available. They are eliminated otherwise.
- Punctuation such as brackets, periods, and commas are removed.
- Stop words (a, an, and, etc.,) are removed.
- Words with special letters and digits are eliminated, as are words that don't only include alphabetical characters.
- Lowercase letters are used for all words.

Translation of emojis is a crucial part of the feature selection. Popular emojis used in sentiment analysis can be translated to plain text using their corresponding Unicode Common Locale Data Repository (CLDR) meaning. The Unicode chart offers a list of the emoji character, codes, and meanings. For example, 😄 has the code U+1F604 and means smiling face. Similarly, ✌ has the code U+0270C which means victory hand. A complete list of Unicode for emojis is available at "http://unicode.org/emoji/charts/full-emoji-list.html" for reference. Translation of emojis helps us to capture the sentiment without losing the original context. The following diagram indicates the steps involved in the feature engineering of eWOM (**Figure 2** and **Table 1**).

The converted plain text may not be a meaningful English sentence but it captures the original sentiment and context. This could be applied as an input vector to ML algorithms. Following are examples of a few plain texts extracted from eWOM.

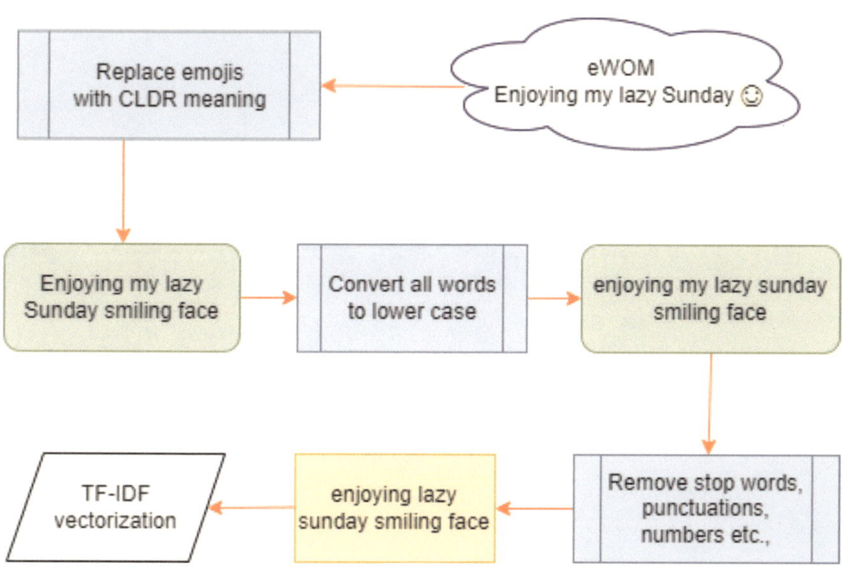

Figure 2.
Feature engineering of eWOM.

No	eWOM	Plain text
1	The market seems crashed! My money is already in the loss... 🙁	the market seems crashed my money already lost a sad face
2	Hey folks the Samsung Galaxy M12 is the best in this price range ✌!!	folks samsung galaxy best price range victory hand
3	People are urging for relief from gundarj, terror & hypocrisy of leaders 🙁	people urging relief gundarj, terror hypocrisy leaders sad face
4	Am afraid the emperor's experiments will continue with a great cost to the nation 😢	afraid the emperor's experiments will continue great cost the nation crying face
5	Everyone crying for #cryptoban. Me who never invested in cryptocurrency 😆	everyone crying crypto ban me never invested cryptocurrency smiling face

Table 1.
Sentences extracted from eWOM.

The extracted plain text is given as input to an automatic system that uses a machine learning algorithm for classification. The automatic system is defined as follows.

Sentiment polarity classification system M is a quadruple

$$M = \{\alpha, \lambda, \delta, \varphi\} \quad (3)$$

where
$\alpha = \{e_1, e_2, \ldots e_n\}$ is a set of messages from social media,
$\lambda = |e_i - e_j|$ is a function that calculates the similarity score of messages,
δ →an algorithm to classify the sentiment polarity, and
$\varphi = \{S_p, S_n, S_o\}$ is a set of output labels: positive, negative, and neutral.

For a given input in α, the algorithm δ produces an output label in φ with the help of the function the following diagram shows the overview of the sentiment classification machine (**Figure 3**).

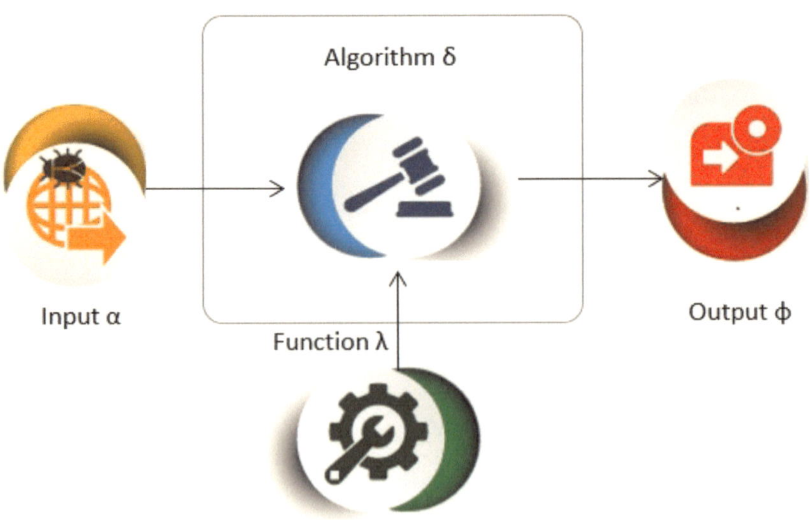

Figure 3.
Sentiment polarity classification system.

The sentiment polarity of social media messages can be efficiently predicted by an artificial intelligence system if we identify the right choice for

1. Function to calculate the similarity score of two messages.

2. A machine learning algorithm for classification.

We will discuss the selection of algorithms for these two tasks in detail in the following sections.

4. Similarity score of messages

Machine learning algorithms mainly work on numerical input vectors. It is essential to convert the pre-processed text to a numerical vector for algorithms to predict the sentiment polarity correctly. The ML model is trained with labeled data sets for positive, negative, and neutral messages. A well-trained model predicts the sentiment polarity of incoming messages by comparing it with members of the training data set. Comparing two messages and giving a numerical score on how similar they are being important for high accuracy. TF-IDF ("Term Frequency-Inverse Document Frequency") is a vectorization approach used widely in text processing. This approach examines the relative frequency of terms in a text via an inverse percentage of the phrase throughout the full corpus of documents [3, 4]. It works well for text categorization or making it possible for machines to interpret input words represented as numbers. In TF-IDF, the same texts must result in a closer vector. TF-IDF is the multiplicative product of the Term Frequency and Inverse Document Frequency scores of the word.

TF represents the "number of times the word appears in the doc / Total number of words in the document.

$$\text{IDF} = \ln\ (\text{Number of documents/Number of documents the word appears in}).$$

$$\text{TF-IDF} = \text{TF}^*\,\text{IDF} \tag{4}$$

The phrase is rarer and vice versa, depending on the TF-IDF score. A smaller score between the documents indicates that they are highly similar to each other. A score of 0 indicates that the papers are entirely equal. Following is an illustration of TF-IDF score calculation using two simple sentences.

Document 1: It is going to rain today.

Document 2: Today I am not going outside.

Word	Count
going	2
today	2
rain	1
outside	1
i	1

Word	Count
am	1
is	1
it	1
to	1
not	1

Table 2.
Word count.

Step 1: Tokenize the words and count their frequency (**Table 2**).
Step 2: Find Term Frequency "(TF).

$$\text{TF} = (\text{Number of times the word appears in the document})/(\text{Total no.of words in a document}) \tag{5}$$

Word	Document 1	Document 2
going	0.17	0.17
today	0.17	0.17
rain	0.17	0
outside	0	0.17
i	0	0.17
am	0	0.17
is	0.17	0
it	0.17	0
to	0.17	0
not	0	0.17

Table 3.
Term frequency.

(See **Table 3**).
Step 3: Find IDF for documents.

$$\text{IDF} = \text{Log}[(\text{Number of documents})/(\text{Number of documents containing the word})] \tag{6}$$

Word	IDF value	IDF (in decimal)
going	$\log_2(2/2)$	0
today	$\log_2(2/2)$	0
rain	$\log_2(2/1)$	1
outside	$\log_2(2/1)$	1
i	$\log_2(2/1)$	1
am	$\log_2(2/1)$	1

Word	IDF value	IDF (in decimal)
is	$\log_2(2/1)$	1
it	$\log_2(2/1)$	1
to	$\log_2(2/1)$	1
not	$\log_2(2/1)$	1

Table 4.
Inverse document frequency.

(See **Table 4**).

Step 4: Calculate TF-IDF for each word.

$$\text{TF-IDF} = \text{TF}^* \text{IDF} \tag{7}$$

Word	Document 1	Document 2
going	0	0
today	0	0
rain	0.17	0
outside	0	0.17
i	0	0.17
am	0	0.17
is	0.17	0
it	0.17	0
to	0.17	0
not	0	0.17

Table 5.
TF-IDF for two documents.

(See **Table 5**).

To measure the similarity between these 2 documents, we need a distance metric. Hamming distance is suitable to measure the distance between column vectors.

Hamming distance is used usually with boolean or string vectors, detecting the points where the vectors do not match. While comparing two vectors of equal length, it is the number of positions in which the values are different. It is also known as the overlap metric.

Now let's use hamming distance to measure the distance between the documents (**Table 6**).

Word	Document 1	Document 2
going	0	0
today	0	0
rain	0.17	0
outside	0	0.17

Word	Document 1	Document 2
i	0	0.17
am	0	0.17
is	0.17	0
it	0.17	0
to	0.17	0
not	0	0.17

Table 6.
Hamming distance between Document 1 and 2.

$$\lambda(\mathrm{doc}1, \mathrm{doc}2) = 8 \tag{8}$$

We observe that these two documents have only two words in common. Hamming distance of TF-IDF is eight. The similarity score generated by our algorithm is a good metric to measure the distance between documents. Two similar documents will have a score of zero. A non-zero score indicates their distance. Having converted the input to a numerical vector and identified a distance metric, we can now use a machine-learning algorithm for sentiment polarity classification.

5. Sentiment classification using machine learning

An identification task for sentiment polarity is usually defined as a classification problem, where a classifier is fed a text and outputs a label, like "positive, negative, or neutral". In general, supervised and unsupervised learning techniques may be used to

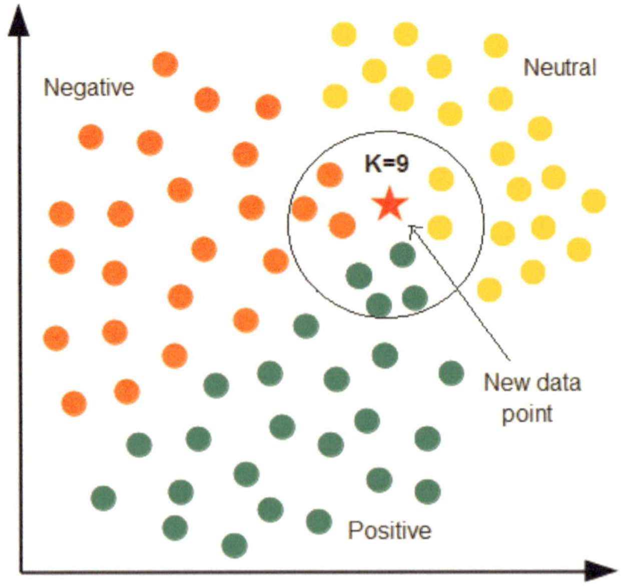

Figure 4.
KNN classification with k = 9.

classify text using a machine learning methodology. Many tagged documents are used in the supervised approaches. Unsupervised approaches are employed when it is challenging to find these labeled training documents. Since thousands of messages of emitted every minute on social media, we can manually label a few thousand and use them for supervised learning. A training data set consisting of three labels namely, positive, negative, and neutral is prepared by picking messages from social media sites like Twitter, Facebook, etc. Only the training documents that are most similar to the incoming document are used by the machine learning algorithm to label it. Popular text classification algorithms include K-Nearest Neighbor (KNN). With the help of supervised learning, this method divides objects into one of the predetermined categories of a sample group. Here we will see how KNN can be used to classify sentiment polarity. If we represent the numerical vectors as points in a diagram, then the training data set will look like this (**Figure 4**).

It is trained with a set of labeled data sets. The label of incoming input is predicted based on the majority voting of its neighbors. The algorithm can be described below.

Algorithm: KNN classification

---

1. *Calculate the distance from the query data item to the labeled data items.*

2. *Order the labeled samples by increasing distance.*

3. *Using accuracy, determine the k nearest neighbours that are the heuristically optimal number. Cross-validation is used to accomplish this.*

4. *Assign a class label to the query example based on majority voting (neighbors).*

5. *A confusion matrix may be used as a tool to check the KNN classification algorithm's accuracy.*

We have three clusters for the labels namely positive, negative, and neutral. During training, labeled data items form the clusters based on the distance from their neighbors. A new data point is assigned a label by picking up nine neighbors and their majority voting.

5.1 Popular algorithms for classification

We have seen how KNN supervised learning method could be applied used for sentiment polarity classification. However, there are few other machine learning algorithms. Researchers can experiment with the following algorithms and choose the right choice based on performance.

XG boost: Extreme Gradient Boosting is referred to as XGBoost. The GBDT ("Gradient-Boosted Decision Tree") ML approach is scalable and distributed. It offers parallel tree boosting and is the most effective ML technique for classification and regression issues.

Support vector machines (SVM): SVM is a supervised method in which the learning method examines the data and finds patterns. We display the data as points in an "n-dimensional" space. The value of every attribute is then connected to a specific coordinate, which facilitates categorization.

Naive bayes(NB): NB is depending on Bayes' Theorem, an approach for determining conditional probability on the basis of previous information and the naive belief that each attribute is independent of the others. The greatest advantage of Naive Bayes is that it works quite well even with small amounts of training data, whereas the majority of ML algorithms rely on huge amounts of training data.

Convolutional neural networks (CNN): Deep learning is gaining popularity due to enhanced chip processing capabilities (GPU units), much cheaper hardware costs, and major advancements in ML methods. Deep neural network design was first used by researchers to assess document similarity. A series of word embeddings constructed from data sets used as inputs to train a CNN-based representation learning model may also be utilized to classify the sentiment polarity.

5.2 Popular performance metrics for classification

The performance of a machine learning algorithm needs to be evaluated before selecting the model for real-world applications. Our sentiment analysis is a classification problem. The results of any classification algorithm can be evaluated by creating a confusion matrix and popular metrics. The following table shows the confusion matrix for a "binary classification" model (**Table 7**).

Based on the elements of the confusion matrix, a set of metrics is generally calculated for assessing the performance of the classification model.

5.2.1 Accuracy and error rate

A classification model's quality may be assessed using these key metrics. A "true positive, a false positive, a true negative, and a false negative", respectively, are denoted as TP, FP, TN, and FN. Following are definitions for the terms Accuracy and Error Rate in classification.

$$\text{Accuracy} = \frac{(\text{TP} + \text{TN})}{\text{N}}, \text{Error Rate} = \frac{(\text{FP} + \text{FN})}{\text{N}} \tag{9}$$

where *N* indicates the total number of samples. Clearly, we have Error Rate = 1 Accuracy.

5.2.2 Recall, F1 score, and precision

These are also the main metrics for unbalanced test sets, and they are applied more frequently than error rate or accuracy. For binary classification, precision, as well as recall, are specified below. The harmonic mean of recall and accuracy is the F1 score.

	Predicted values	
Actual values	True Positive (TP)	False Negative (FN)
	False Positive (FP)	True Negative (TN)

Table 7.
Confusion matrix for classification model.

The F1 score is best when it is 1 (perfect recall and precision), and it is worse when it is 0.

$$\text{Precision} = \frac{\text{TP}}{(\text{TP} + \text{FP})}, \text{Recall} = \frac{\text{TP}}{(\text{TP} + \text{FN})}, \text{F1-Score} = \frac{2^* \text{Prec}^* \text{Rec}}{(\text{Prec} + \text{Rec})} \quad (10)$$

We may always calculate recall and precision for every class label in multi-class classification problems, assess each class label's performance individually, or simply average the numbers to obtain the overall recall and precision. The average for the three classifications positive, negative, and neutral in our situation may be determined.

6. Applications of social media sentiment analysis

Traditional polling may be replaced by AI-based social media analysis, which is also a more affordable way for decision-makers to comprehend the situation and address any emerging crises. Social media is used by the public proactively to express their sentiment and opinion. People post millions of messages every minute on social media. If these messages are analyzed and opinion is extracted, it will help decision-

No.	Twitter eWOM	Sentiment
1	Future generations will continue to be inspired by their sacrifice for our motherland👏	Positive
2	We appreciate and respect your sacrifices, and we will always be grateful for them.🙏	Positive
3	If you carry your childhood with you, you never become older 😊	Positive
4	The government has officially proclaimed that India is currently under a state of emergency as a result of attacks on farmers🙈	Negative
5	A paranoid, vindictive administration won't let farmers survive😞.	Negative

Table 8.
Sentiment classification by automatic system.

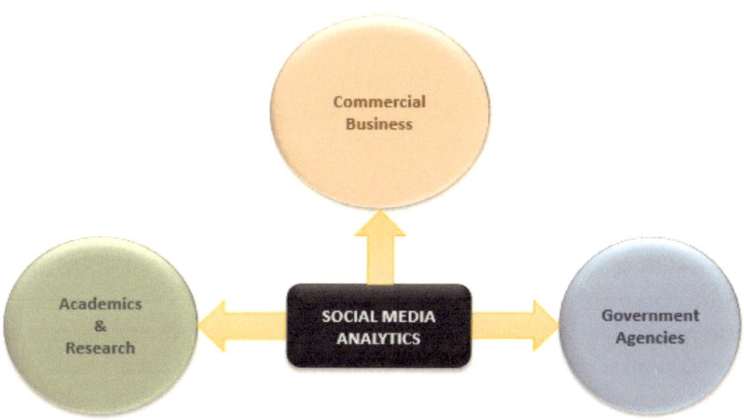

Figure 5.
Real world applications of social media analytics.

makers to quickly respond to any crisis. Following are examples of sentiments captured by an automatic system from Twitter (**Table 8**).

Results are convincing in the possibility to replace manual sentiment classification with automatic systems. The experimental results show promising output and can be used by online marketing companies, and government agencies for decision-making [5]. Online advertisement agencies can use this study for effectively targeted marketing campaigns. On the other hand, Government organizations could know how the public is affected by a policy or decision and then decide how to respond to public opinion. It has many applications in the real world. The above diagram shows the areas where social media analytics is finding its applications (**Figure 5**).

It allows business organizations to determine how consumers feel about their brands and products, identify how they feel about advertising efforts, and generally track which way the wind is blowing. Social media analytics helps commercial organizations in the following areas:

- Derive customer sentiment towards products and services.
- Understand conversations - what is being told and how it is being received.
- Spot trends related to brands and service offerings.
- Find the high-value components of a service or product.
- Assess the reaction to messaging on social media and other channels.
- Find out what the competition is saying and its efficacy.
- Learn how third-party partners and channels may impact performance.

7. Conclusion

The AI strategy produced greater results when it came to categorizing eWOMs' sentiments based on polarity. The two-step process, namely Feature Extractor and Machine Learning, eliminates the main difficulty in employing NLP tools to comprehend social media communications. Commercial enterprises may increase accuracy and acquire greater insights when assessing customer comments and complaints by employing a centralized sentiment analysis system. The following are some general advantages of AI-based sentiment analysis:

Sorting data at scale: It is difficult and time-consuming to manually review thousands of tweets, customer service discussions, or survey responses. AI-based sentiment analysis enables businesses to analyze massive amounts of data economically and efficiently.

Real-time analysis: Organizations may immediately detect dangerous circumstances on a real-time basis with the use of social media analysis and take action before consumers start to leave. Text sentiment labeling is highly subjective and is affected by personal experiences, viewpoints, and opinions. Words such as extremely, quiet, most, etc. are examples of intensifiers. These are the terms that affect how the adjacent non-neutral terms feel. They may be broken down into 2 categories: those that raise the intensity of feeling (very, very much) and those that tone it down (little). Through a rule-based method, determining the strength of an emotion might not be straightforward. The AI-based model may still be improved to determine the level of emotion intensity.

Author details

K. Victor Rajan
Atlantic International University, Hawaii, USA

*Address all correspondence to: victor@jts.co.in

References

[1] Iriani A, Hendry, Manongga DHF, Chen R-C. Mining public opinion on radicalism in social media via sentiment analysis. International Journal of Innovative Computing, Information and Control. 2020;**16**(5):1787-1800

[2] Adnan D, Fei S. Feature selection for sentiment analysis based on content and syntax models. Decision Support Systems. 2012;**53**:704-711

[3] Qaiser S, Ali R. Text mining: Use of TF-IDF to examine the relevance of words to documents. International Journal of Computer Applications. 2018; **181**:25-29

[4] Ravi K, Ravi V. Sentiment classification of Hinglish text. In: Third International Conference in Recent Advances in Information Technology. RAIT-2016. 2016. pp. 641-645. DOI: 10.1109/RAIT.2016.7507974

[5] Ravi K, Ravi V. A survey on opinion mining and sentiment analysis: Tasks, approaches and applications. Knowledge-Based Systems. 2015;**89**: 14-46. ISSN: 0950-7051

Chapter 5

Citizen Sentiment Analysis

Yohei Seki

Abstract

Recently, the co-creation process between citizens and local governments has become increasingly significant as a mechanism for addressing administrative concerns, such as public facility maintenance, disaster response, and overall administrative improvement driven by citizen feedback. Social media platforms have been recognized as effective tools to facilitate this co-creation process. Compared to traditional methods like surveys and public comment solicitations, social listening is deemed superior for obtaining authentic and naturally articulated citizen voices. However, there is a noticeable lack of research concerning the gathering of opinions specifically related to municipal issues via platforms like X (Twitter). This study seeks to address this gap by presenting an original methodology for analyzing citizen opinions through the deployment of large language models. Utilizing these models, we introduce three distinct applications based on our framework, each considering a different opinion typology. We demonstrate that our approach enables the analysis and comparison of citizen sentiments across various cities in relation to common political issues, tailoring the analysis to diverse goal types. The results of this research not only contribute to the understanding of citizen engagement via social media but also provide valuable insights into potential applications of large language models for municipal-related opinion analysis.

Keywords: sentiment analysis, social listening, X (Twitter), citizen engagement, large language models

1. Introduction

Citizen cooperation has become indispensable in recent years in local government administration as a way to reduce administrative costs. The advent of communication through social networking sites (SNS) has enabled citizens to identify and tackle administrative issues such as the repair of public facilities, graffiti removal, and disaster countermeasures, akin to the Open311 platform[1].

However, citizen participation is paramount in the decision-making process of local government administration. Traditional methods of collecting opinions, such as questionnaires and public comments, have inherent limitations, including a limited participant pool and the influence of vocal individuals. As a solution, the potential of public opinion analysis using SNSs like X (formerly known as Twitter) has been acknowledged.

[1] https://www.open311.org/

For an authentic collection of citizen opinions, it is crucial to garner opinions from specific municipalities through social media platforms. While participation in region-specific SNSs might be low, platforms like X with a larger user base can serve as a useful tool for collecting and analyzing citizen opinions on administrative issues. In Section 3.2, we introduce a strategy to amass citizen sentiment in a specific city.

Given the age group bias in X participation, directly incorporating citizen opinions from X into public administration might not be feasible. Hence, it is crucial to comparatively analyze these opinions with those from other cities. While city comparisons are necessary, there is a dearth of studies that collect and compare tweets from multiple cities using a social listening approach. To address this gap, we introduce a general framework in Section 3. In Sections 4, 5, and 6, we also present research on citizen sentiment across cities through three concrete applications, linking it to real-world scenarios.

While sentiment and polarity analysis have traditionally been used for product reviews and X trends, it is vital to assess citizens' attitudes toward the target of their opinions when analyzing their authentic voices. This requires annotated corpora with detailed information, tailored to the application's goal. We introduce three types of opinion typology in line with the application's objective.

Collecting opinions on specific administrative issues from SNS poses challenges due to the diverse range of topics discussed. It's not only important to collect opinions with relevant keywords but also to consider and analyze them within the context of the administrative issue at hand. As facility and event names related to administrative issues vary from city to city, creating tailored training data for opinion analysis for each city and administrative topic is desirable, albeit cost-intensive.

This chapter details the research conducted to address these challenges, emphasizing the use of large-scale language models and fine-tuning approaches for citizen opinion analysis. Our work builds on the studies by [1, 2] and explores the application of these methods in citizen sentiment analysis.

2. Related works

Sentiment analysis or opinion mining has been conducted for a long time [3]. The first target document genre is newspaper [4], product review [5], or blogs [6]. Then, social media such as Twitter (now called X) became the main target to conduct public opinion analysis [7, 8]. Recently, social media sentiment analysis has been extended to applications focused on public service [9]. In this section, we discuss two types of related works from the two viewpoints as follows: (a) applications of citizen sentiment analysis and (2) opinion typology used for citizen sentiment analysis.

2.1 Application of citizen sentiment analysis

Citizen sentiment analysis has been a focal point since 2010 [8]. Subsequently, researchers have explored citizen comments in various domains, such as urban projects [10], reactions to government secretary accounts [11], and responses to the COVID-19 pandemic [12], all of which have proven to be effective target domains.

Alizadeh et al. [10] conducted research to collect citizen opinions for informing local government decision-making. They gathered tweets using project-specific hashtags or query keywords. Hubert et al. [11], on the other hand, explored citizen comments in response to tweets posted by five secretaries of the Government of Mexico.

In contrast, our method focuses on collecting more generalized citizen opinions relevant to political issues across different cities. We collected citizen comments based on the city using the approach described in Section 3.2. Additionally, we extracted citizen responses using broader query keywords related to political issues, including those pertaining to COVID-19 infections. This approach allows us to gain insights into the broader sentiments and opinions of citizens across cities on various political matters, offering valuable information for decision-making and policy analysis.

2.2 Opinion typology used for citizen sentiment analysis

Opinion analysis on Twitter (X) has attracted significant attention from numerous researchers, primarily focusing on the classification of emotions in tweets [13–15]. Dini et al. [13], for instance, challenged the conventional assumption that all tweets inherently express opinions and consequently introduced a task for identifying non-opinionated tweets. In contrast, Jabreel et al. [14] designed a classification task to identify a single emotion and proposed an attention-based technique for recognizing multiple emotions within a tweet.

These pioneering studies have advanced Twitter opinion analysis, exploring diverse aspects such as emotion classification and identification of opinion-expressing tweets. However, they primarily focus on polarity [16] and emotion classification [13–15, 17], which we argue, may not fully represent the breadth and complexity of citizens' opinions expressed on X.

In response to this gap, we propose a unique framework for citizen sentiment analysis. After presenting a common framework for this in Section 3, we introduce a set of opinion typologies tailored for different applications. These include eliciting feedback from citizens (Section 4), comparing policy discussion trends with city council members (Section 5), and estimating social connections among citizens (Section 6). We argue that these typologies offer a more nuanced understanding of citizen sentiment, enabling the extraction and organization of citizen feedback by analyzing tweets from a variety of perspectives.

3. Citizen sentiment analysis framework

3.1 Our framework overview

We present a sentiment analysis framework designed for analyzing citizen comments, consisting of four stages as shown in **Figure 1**.

1. Crawling city-specific citizen tweets,

2. Classifying comments using an opinion typology applied via large language models,

3. Consolidating opinions based on assigned labels, and

4. Comparing temporal civic sentiment trends across cities.

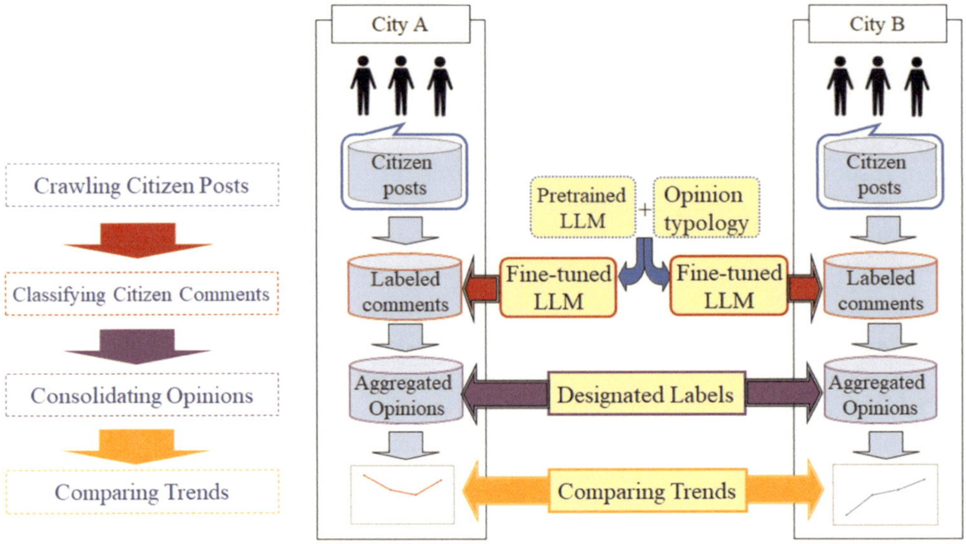

Figure 1.
Our citizen sentiment analysis framework.

The framework begins with the collection of city-specific tweets. These tweets are then categorized using a custom opinion typology implemented via a fine-tuned large language model. This typology, informed by the application's purpose, allows for a nuanced analysis of public sentiment. Next, we consolidate the categorized opinions based on their assigned labels within specific timeframes for each city. Finally, we visualize and compare the temporal trends of civic sentiment across different cities.

The methodology of the tweet collection stage is detailed in Section 3.2. The subsequent stages are discussed in relation to three applications: extracting civic feedback (Section 4), comparing citizens' and city councilors' opinions (Section 5), and estimating social capital (Section 6).

3.2 Crawling citizen comments

In recent years, X (Twitter) has become a prominent platform for capturing citizen sentiments and opinions. Extracting relevant accounts from this vast social media platform is essential to gain valuable insights into local issues. This section introduces a method for efficiently crawling citizen comments on X, with a focus on city-level residents. To crawl citizen comments, we have proposed a methodology to collect citizen accounts from X using profile information [18].

3.2.1 Seeded resident account collection

We define a method to collect citizen accounts by leveraging profile information. This method involves matching district names with user profiles to gather seeded resident accounts. Japan's Twitter user profile search service[2] plays a crucial role in extracting the initial set of seed accounts.

[2] https://twpro.jp/

3.2.2 Account extension

To enhance the scope of our extracted accounts, we propose extensions based on followers' characteristics. These extensions are subjected to three specific constraints: the maximum number of followers (3000), the maximum number of friends (4000), and the minimum number of followers of the seed account. The first two constraints were set to exclude famous people or bot accounts. By applying these constraints, we ensure that the extended accounts remain relevant and representative of city-level residents.

3.2.3 Preliminary experiment: Tsukuba City

For evaluation purposes, we conducted a preliminary experiment in Tsukuba City, Japan, a city with a population of approximately 250,000. In this experiment, we targeted accounts relevant to Tsukuba City and extended them based on twice the number of followers (i.e., the followers of followers of followers). Additionally, we randomly selected 200 citizen accounts and manually annotated their career types.

3.2.4 Results and discussion

The results of the manual annotations are presented in **Figure 2**, indicating a substantial representation of residential users among the extracted accounts. This observation aligns with Tsukuba City's demographic, which mainly consists of students due to its status as a academic city. The proposed X account extraction method proves effective in gathering citizen comments from city-level residents. By leveraging profile information and applying follower-based extensions, we obtained a significant dataset of valid residential users. The method's reliability and applicability are demonstrated through the case study in Tsukuba City, providing valuable insights for understanding local opinions and sentiments on X and other social media platforms.

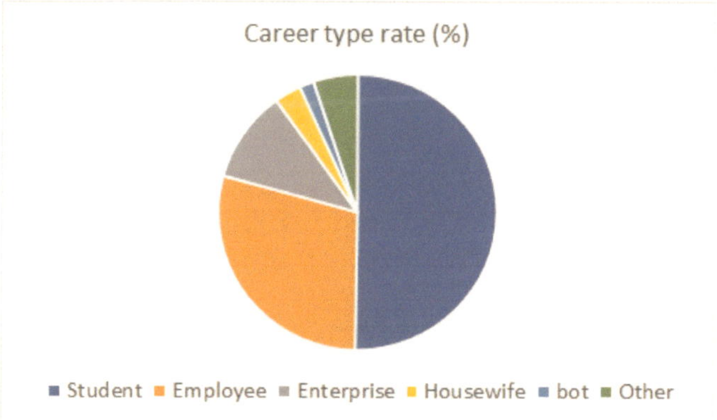

Figure 2.
Career type rate in Tsukuba city.

4. Application (1): extraction of citizen feedback

In this section, we describe the application to extract citizen feedback for local government administration. This work is based on our paper [1].

4.1 Goal

Obtaining citizens' feedback is crucial for enhancing local government and nongovernmental customer service initiatives and mitigating infectious disease spread, thereby promoting a vibrant social life. Current systems, like public comment platforms and council membership competitions, have limitations in attracting sufficient residents and may be biased toward certain attitudes. To address this, a new method is proposed for acquiring a large volume of unbiased and experienced citizen feedback.

The study introduces a novel approach to extract citizens' opinions from X, where users express diverse thoughts daily. Unlike conventional studies focusing on polarity and emotion classification, this research adopts appraisal theory [19] to categorize various opinions, thereby enabling a comprehensive analysis. A large language model (LLM) is utilized to analyze tweets from multiple perspectives and extract citizen feedback based on specific conditions.

By adopting this new approach, local governments and nongovernmental entities can obtain a diverse range of citizen opinions, leading to better policy guidance and service improvement. The proposed method enables policymakers to gain valuable insights into public sentiment during the pandemic, fostering more effective and inclusive decision-making processes.

4.2 Opinion typology for extracting citizen feedback

This study introduces a novel methodology for gleaning citizens' opinions from the prominent social media platform, X. Capitalizing on the platform's user interaction diversity, we conveniently capture a broad range of civic sentiments. Our method hinges on three attitude categories derived from appraisal theory: affect (e.g., satisfaction or dissatisfaction), judgment of behavior (e.g., staff performance evaluation),

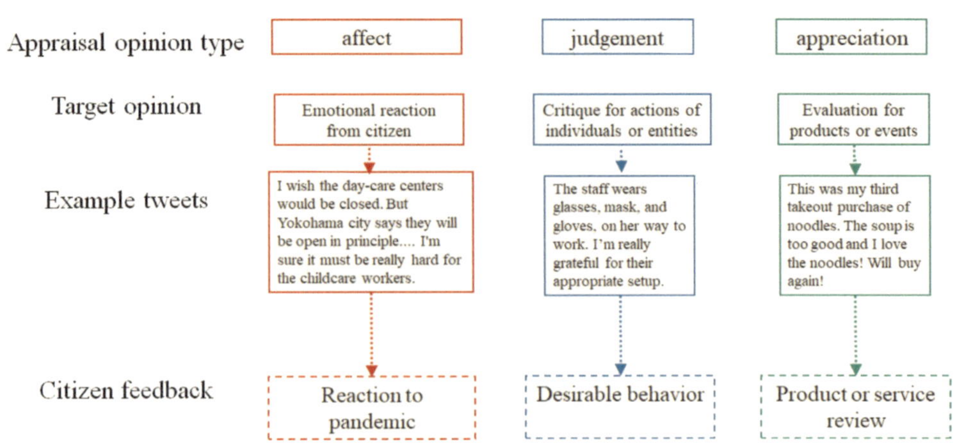

Figure 3.
Appraisal opinion type for extracting citizen feedback.

Opinion type	Value
Polarity	positive, negative, neutral, N/A
Appraisal	affect, judgment, appreciation, N/A
Communication	speculation, suggestion, question, request, N/A

Table 1.
Opinion typology used in our study [1].

and appreciation (e.g., assessment of facilities or products). This approach empowers us to probe into the varied opinions expressed by citizens on X, differentiating feedback according to informational needs, as depicted in **Figure 3**.

To overcome the limitations of existing studies, which often overlook opinions and attitudes toward society, we propose analyzing citizens' opinions from multiple viewpoints, including appraisal opinion types, while also examining their chronological appearance frequency. By doing so, we aim to better understand citizens' opinions and attitudes toward society within specific time ranges during the COVID-19 pandemic. This comprehensive approach will yield a more holistic and nuanced understanding of public sentiment, thereby aiding policymakers and researchers in developing effective strategies and policies to address societal concerns.

Additionally, we address the absence of linguistic modality and speech act theory categories in appraisal theory by introducing the "communication opinion type" viewpoint. Furthermore, within the "attitude" category of appraisal theory, the value of the category combines both positive and negative opinions without distinction. To rectify this, we define the "polarity" viewpoint.

In summary, the opinion typology used in this study is presented in **Table 1**.

4.3 Methodology

We used a common LLM to simultaneously estimate the three viewpoints (polarity/appraisal/communication opinion types) of the opinion unit. The three viewpoints of the opinion units refer to the same opinion. Therefore, we assumed that these estimation tasks relate to each other and show their effectiveness of the multitask learning approach [20] for estimation tasks. By performing multiple tasks concurrently using a shared model, we performed that higher F1-scores were achieved compared to independent task performance significantly. This multitasks learning approach enhances opinion extraction accuracy. In the first paper [1], we used BERT model [21] as a pretrained LLM. In the later version [22], we updated our model using T5 model [23], because it was an LLM which leveraged a unified approach to treat all NLP tasks as a "text-to-text" problem, and was also suitable for multitask learning.

In addition, comparing citizen opinions across different cities is crucial to discern whether sentiments expressed are specific to the analyzed city or shared among citizens in diverse locations. However, variations in municipal policies and hospitality services necessitate creating another data for training citizen opinion extraction models in each city of interest. Creating training data for all cities incurs high costs, rendering such an approach unrealistic.

To address this challenge, in our work [22], we proposed a method for extracting citizen opinions in a target city by leveraging data from a city with pre-constructed

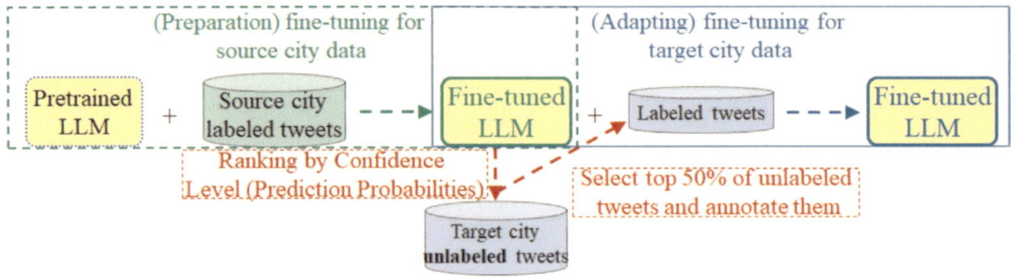

Figure 4.
Selecting comments for labeling in target with confidence level.

training data (referred to as the source city) alongside a relatively small amount of data from the target city. Specifically, we utilized the confidence levels of predictions made on the target city's data by a model fine-tuned on the source city's data to effectively select the target city's training data. The proposed method reduces the cost of creating training data to approximately half of that required for extracting citizen opinions from an entirely new city. The steps of our proposed method are illustrated in **Figure 4**.

In our experiments, annotating the top 50% of unlabeled tweets with confidence levels and applying fine-tuning to adapt to the target city outperformed methods that randomly selected 50% or the bottom 50% of unlabeled tweets significantly in terms of F1 score. Additionally, we observed no significant difference in estimation accuracy in terms of F1-score when compared to the estimation of opinion types using 100% of unlabeled data in the target cities as labeled training data for fine-tuning as an upper bound. Therefore, this approach allows us to discern sentiments across different cities more efficiently and cost-effectively.

4.4 Comparing citizen feedback across different cities

In this study, we conducted an analysis to extract citizens' opinions specific to target cities, using nursery school services as an example, in the government-designated cities of Yokohama and Sapporo in Japan. Specifically, we focused on citizens' opinions expressing parental sentiments in Yokohama during the early period of the COVID-19 disaster in April 2020. The results revealed that Yokohama citizens who are raising children expressed dissatisfaction ("affect") with the city's policy to open daycare centers during this period. These opinions were specific to Yokohama residents and hold potential value for the city in improving its policies.

In contrast, the opinions of Sapporo citizens displayed a noteworthy trend, with a significant proportion consisting of evaluations ("appreciation") concerning various aspects, including events and things. This allowed us to extract opinions expressing confusion about the current situation of nursery schools remaining open during the COVID-19 pandemic, as well as opinions about specific events, such as cases of discrimination against infected people occurring at nursery schools. These tweets provided valuable insights for proposing policy improvements, as they shed light on specific events that citizens were troubled by and allowed us to discern areas where improvements could be made.

Our analysis highlighted the significance of extracting location-specific citizen opinions, as it provides valuable feedback for local governments to enhance policy decision-making processes and address citizens' concerns effectively.

5. Application (2): comparison of stances for citizens with city councilors

In this section, we introduce the application of citizens' stances analysis for political issues to compare with the stances of city councilors, with referring to [2].

5.1 Goal

In local governance, analyzing the disparities in citizens' and city councilors' opinions on political matters is vital for representing the people's will in politics and fostering citizen engagement. With the abundance of citizens expressing their views on X and city councils sharing meeting minutes as open data on the web, digital archives offer valuable resources for opinion analysis.

In this study, we propose and evaluate a method for automatically predicting stances in citizen tweets and city council minutes, subsequently aggregating the percentages of "favor" or "against" for each city. By comparing the results for each city, we ascertain the distinct characteristics of citizens and city councilors, underscoring the significance and efficacy of our approach.

5.2 Attribute type for comparing stances

In our study, the dataset constructed may encompass texts unrelated to political issues. To address this, we performed annotations not only for "stance" but also for "relevance" to the political matter. Additionally, for a more in-depth opinion analysis, we further annotated two attributes: "usefulness," indicating whether the texts include specific information and evidence, and "regional dependency," determining if they are connected to the place of residence. An overview of the attribute typology employed in this research is presented in **Table 2**.

5.3 Methodology

In our dataset, some texts do not explicitly mention political issues but contain opinions on them, while others seem to express opinions on unrelated topics. To achieve accurate stance prediction, it becomes crucial to account for the relevance of the political issue. Thus, in this study, we employed multitask learning [20] to simultaneously train the stance and relevance attributes. Moreover, considering the interconnected nature of the usefulness and regional dependency attributes with relevance, we also employed multitask learning, training them together with relevance. By adopting this multitask approach, we enhance the model's ability to capture the intricacies and dependencies among attributes, leading to more accurate and

Attribute Type	Value
Stance	favor, against, N/A
Usefulness	yes, N/A
Regional dependency	yes, N/A
Relevance	yes, N/A

Table 2.
Attribute typology used in our study [2].

comprehensive predictions of stance, relevance, usefulness, and regional dependency in citizen tweets and city council minutes.

5.4 Comparing stances across different cities

In this study, we direct our attention to the distribution of stance labels in order to identify valuable citizen and councilor comments related to political issues. By analyzing these labels, we gain insights into the perceptions of individuals concerning various issues. Notably, we conducted a comparative examination of two cities: Osaka and Yokohama, ordinance-designated cities in Japan.

Our findings reveal a significant contrast instances between the citizens and councilors of these two cities. Specifically, individuals from Osaka displayed a notably more positive stance toward the attraction of integrated resorts (IR) in comparison to their counterparts in Yokohama. This disparity in attitudes aligns with the ultimate decision taken by the Yokohama Mayor in 2021 to discontinue the IR attraction. It is essential to note that the timing of this decision postdates the timing of the stance analysis conducted in this research.

These results demonstrate the potential of our approach in extracting valuable insights from citizen and councilor comments, contributing to a better understanding of the prevailing sentiments and opinions surrounding political issues. By focusing on stance labels, we gain a nuanced understanding of the viewpoints held by different stakeholders, allowing us to identify patterns and differences among cities. The contrasting stances observed in Osaka and Yokohama regarding integrated resorts exemplify the effectiveness of our methodology.

6. Application (3): comparing social capital in each city

6.1 Goal

The objective of this research is to provide a quantitative analysis of the intensity of human connections and elucidate the varying degrees of these connections across different cities. In doing so, we posit the potential for municipalities to gauge the strength of their local social ties, thereby enabling local governments to effectively address social isolation in areas with comparatively weaker ties.

This study further quantifies human connection strength during the unprecedented period of the 2020 and 2021 novel COVID-19 pandemic, when social relationships were notably strained. By scrutinizing variations in our calculated values over time, in conjunction with alterations in the prevalence of mood disorders, our investigation aims to unravel the underpinnings of the reported increase in conditions like depression, which have surged during the COVID-19 outbreak and have been inadequately explored in preceding studies.

To achieve these objectives, we leverage social capital [24] – a concept intrinsically linked to the quantification of human connection strength - as a metric, deriving our data from tweets on the social media platform, X. This study seeks to validate the efficacy of an affordable quantification method founded on tweet data, which has been under-explored in comparison to the more traditional, yet costly, quantification approach reliant on questionnaire surveys, widely utilized in conventional research. Note that this is ongoing work and reported in the domestic non-reviewed conference in Japan [25].

6.2 Indicator type for estimating social capital

In our proposed methodology, we initially aggregate tweets from cities at both ends of the spectrum concerning the prevalence of mood disorders, as reported on X.

Subsequently, employing the construct of social capital, we derive two indicators from the assembled tweets, assigning attributes through annotation to formulate a comprehensive dataset. The proposed indicators are delineated as follows:

1. Event and Activity Participation: In alignment with the concept of bridging social capital, this indicator is formulated to represent the extent of event participation among contributors residing in the target cities.

2. Family Ties Intensity: Based on the definition of bonding social capital, this indicator is conceived to articulate the strength of relationships between the contributor and their relatives.

Our indicators are conceptualized based on the bifurcation of social capital as per Putnam [24], who differentiated it into two categories bridging and bonding, each embodying distinct characteristics of human connections.

We assembled tweets from four cities: Mito and Oita, characterized by the highest rates of mood disorder patient increase, and Aomori and Takasaki, marked by the lowest rates. Documents were curated such that each category comprised 500 tweets from the pre-pandemic period and 500 from the pandemic period, yielding a total of 1,000 tweets per category. Thus, the resultant dataset encapsulates approximately 8,000 sentences.

To procure tweets pertinent to each indicator, we gathered tweets spanning June 2018–September 2021, encapsulating both pre-pandemic and pandemic periods, guided by the subsequent search queries:

- Event and Activity Participation

The search query was “participation.”

- Family Ties Intensity

Search queries encompassed “son,” “daughter,” “mother,” “father,” “brother,” “younger brother,” “family,” “husband,” “wife,” “parents,” and so on.

Tweets were collected from 12,927 Mito citizen accounts, 9,026 Oita citizen accounts, 9,784 Aomori citizen accounts, and 9,301 Takasaki citizen accounts. These were retrieved based on profile information from X (Twitter) using Twitter’s Streaming API. The number of tweets collected amounted to 10,083,874 from Mito, 5,823,539 from Oita, 11,177,635 from Aomori, and 6,974,843 from Takasaki. Accordingly, for each city, we culled tweets containing the defined queries so that a sum of 2,000 tweets (1,000 for each indicator) were collected during the specified period. Reposts were omitted, and URLs contained within the tweets were excised. This dataset serves as the foundation for training a classification model for each attribute, individual city, and respective indicator.

In this methodology, we delineate attributes that are uniformly allocated to the degree of connectivity with relatives, in addition to labels denoted to the degree of event participation. Social capital is quantified for each indicator, drawing from tweets associated with the ensuing labels.

6.2.1 Attributes assigned to the level of event participation

- Event Participation: We determine whether the content signifies participation in events such as sports, games, music festivals, and so on. There are four label categories: “currently participating,” “participated in the past,” “not participating,” and “not related.”

- Form of Event Participation: This attribute is ascribed to tweets associated with one of three classifications: “currently participating,” “participated in the past,” or “not participating” in the aforementioned attribute of event participation status. This attribute indicates whether the post user partakes in the event virtually or physically. There are three label types: “online,” “offline,” and “unknown.”

6.2.2 Attributes assigned to the degree of connection with relatives

- Connection Information: We assess whether the content comprises information about relatives linked to the post user. The associated label type is “Yes,” in the contrary case, the label type is “No.” For instance, “Husband of an acquaintance” contains expressions relating to relatives such as “husband,” yet the content does not pertain to the post user’s relatives. Hence, such tweets are evaluated as “No” for the connection information.

- Form of Connection Information: This attribute is assigned exclusively to tweets denoted as “Yes” in the above “connection information” attribute. It discerns whether the interaction between the post user and a related individual is face-to-face or online. There are three label types: “online,” “offline,” and “unknown”.

- Evaluation of Connection: This attribute is conferred solely on tweets labeled as “Yes” in the above “connection information” attribute. Drawing from expressions in the post users, encompassing the sentiments and actions of the post users, we assess the quality of the connection between the post users and the other party. This attribute accounts for the “trust” toward others, a component of social capital, and “reciprocity,” which pertains to relationships of mutual support, such as gift exchange. There are three label types: “positive,” “negative,” and “neutral.”

6.3 Methodology

The model was trained to assign the label of the attributes to each tweet using the labeled annotation corpus with RoBERTa [26]. Then, the labels were assigned to the unlabeled tweets in each city using the model, allowing for the quantification of social capital based on the assigned labels to each tweet.

By assigning labels to a large number of unknown tweets using the proposed method in this study, we calculate correlation coefficients between the number of labeled tweets per month and the number of patients with mood disorders per city in the target cities. The period of analysis was from June 2018 to December 2021. The number of patients with mood disorders per month is calculated using REZULT[3], a medical database provided by Japan System Techniques Corporation (JAST). This data set is based on the receipt data of more than 7 million patients held by JAST, and the number of patients is calculated by ICD-10 code, which is the International Statistical Classification of Diseases, and by region. In order to analyze the data by period, correlation coefficients were calculated for a six-month period, from June 2018 to December 2019 (before COVID-19) and from January 2020 to March 2022 (after COVID-19).

6.4 Correlation of number of labeled tweets and number of patients with mood disorders in cities

During the early COVID-19 pandemic period from January to June 2020, we observed a negative correlation (−0.157 to −0.656) between the number of patients with mood disorders and the count of tweets labeled "currently participating" and "online" in the attribute "forms of event participation." This supports the hypothesis that a higher participation of citizens in events is associated with a decrease in the number of mood disorder cases.

The strong negative correlation case in Aomori city case is depicted in **Figure 5**. Note that Aomori was characterized by the lowest rates of mood disorder patient increase. During this period, numerous tweets discussed online drinking parties and social gatherings, utilizing Zoom for virtual interactions.

The negative correlation coefficient between the number of patients with mood disorders and the count of tweets labeled as "positive" for offline connectedness from January to June 2020 was notably higher (−0.525 to −0.629) in cities. This suggested that kinship ties might have reduced mood disorder patient numbers in early COVID-19 pandemic stages.

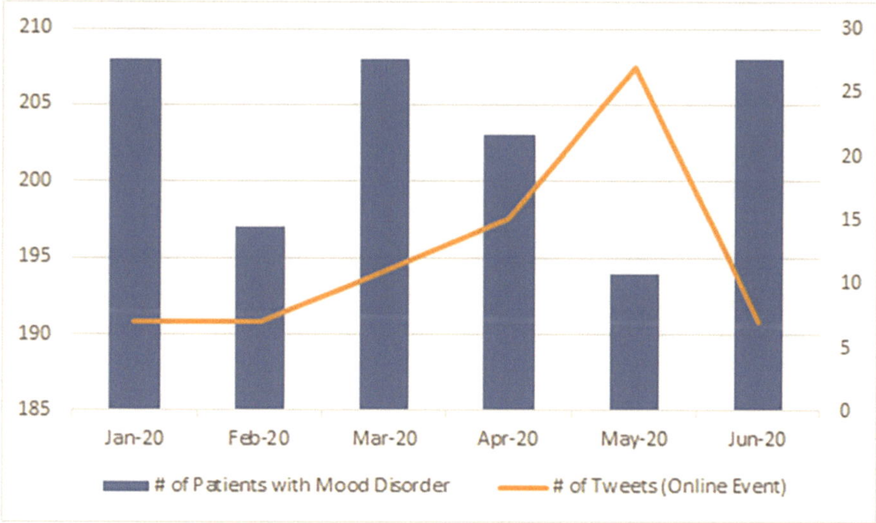

Figure 5.
Negative correlation between # of tweets currently participating in online events and # of patients with mood disorders in Aomori city.

3 https://www.jastlab.jast.jp/rezult_data/

7. Limitations

Our approach exhibits several limitations. Notably, it struggles to analyze opinions that rarely surface on social media. For instance, although restroom locations in offline events constitute an important concern, few users discuss this topic on X. Additionally, due to limited X usage among older demographics, assessing elder-specific issues is challenging. Another complication is distinguishing the impact of non-opinion factors when analyzing real-world problem influences. An example would be assessing the effect of social media rumors on decreasing COVID-19 vaccination rates, considering that inadequate local government services also contribute to this decline. Understanding these limitations is crucial before deploying our proposed methodology for analysis.

8. Conclusions

In this chapter, we presented our methodologies for citizen sentiment analysis using tweets in a specific city, with a focus on three main applications: (1) comparing citizen feedback in multiple cities; (2) comparing the stance of citizens with city councilors; and (3) estimating social capital to affect the number of patients with mood disorder. Our approach encompassed a wide range of political issues, enabling us to compare citizen responses and connections across various cities by collecting tweets specific to each location. To prove the generality of our framework, we introduced multiple opinion typologies according to the application goal. Moreover, to enhance the accuracy and efficiency of extracting citizen comments, we incorporated a multitask learning framework based on LLMs.

Looking ahead, we plan to construct a conversation agent in each city to adapt generative AI to each city, by creating specific instructions in each city. This application plays a role as a virtual citizen, and holds significant promise for facilitating targeted interventions to enhance community well-being. By bridging the gap between digital interactions and real-life connections, our research contributes to a more comprehensive understanding of citizen sentiments and lays the groundwork for more informed decision-making in public administration.

Acknowledgements

This work was partially supported by the Japanese Society for the Promotion of Science Grant-in-Aid for Scientific Research (B) (#23H03686) and Grant-in-Aid for Challenging Exploratory Research (#22 K19822).

Author details

Yohei Seki
Institute of Library, Information, and Media Science, University of Tsukuba, Japan

*Address all correspondence to: yohei@slis.tsukuba.ac.jp

References

[1] Ishida T, Seki Y, Kashino W, Kando N. Extracting citizen feedback from social media by appraisal opinion type viewpoint. Journal of Natural Language Processing. 2022;**29**(2): 416-442. DOI: 10.5715/jnlp.29.416 [Accessed: 1 July 2023]

[2] Senoo K, Seki Y, Kashino W, Kando N. Visualization of the gap between the stances of citizens and City Councilors on political issues. In: Tseng Y-H, Katsurai M, Nguyen HN, editors. From Born-Physical to Born-Virtual: Augmenting Intelligence in Digital Libraries, Lecture Notes in Computer Science. Vol. 13636. Hanoi, Vietnam: Springer; 2022. pp. 73-89. DOI: 10.1007/978-3-031-21756-2_6 [Accessed: 1 July 2023]

[3] Pang B, Lee L. Opinion Mining and Sentiment Analysis. Boston: Now Publishers Inc; 2008

[4] Wiebe JM, Wilson T, Bruce RF, Bell M, Martin M. Learning subjective language. Computational Linguistics. 2005;**30**(3):277-308. Available from: https://aclanthology.org/J04-3002.pdf [Accessed: 1 July 2023]

[5] Blitzer J, Dredze M, Pereira F. Biographies, bollywood, boom-boxes and blenders: domain adaptation for sentiment classification. In: Proceedings of the 45th Annual Meeting of the Association of Computational Linguistics (ACL), Prague, Czech Republic. 2007. pp. 440-447. Available from: https://aclanthology.org/P07-1056/ [Accessed: 1 July 2023]

[6] Macdonald C, Ounis I. The TREC Blogs06 collection: creating and analysing a blog test collection. Technical report TR-2006-224. Department of Computing Science, University of Glasgow: 2006. Available from: http://terrierteam.dcs.gla.ac.uk/publications/macdonald06creating.pdf [Accessed: 1 July 2023]

[7] Martinez-Camara E, Martin-Valdivia MT, Urena-Lopez LA, Montejo-Raez AR. Sentiment analysis in twitter. Natural Language Engineering. 2014;**20**(1):1-28. DOI: 10.1017/S1351324912000332 [Accessed: 1 July 2023]

[8] Stylios G, Christodoulakis D, Besharat J, Vonitsanou M, Kotrotsos I, Koumpouri A, et al. Public opinion Mining for Governmental Decisions. Electronic Journal of e-Government. 2010;**8**(2):203-214

[9] Verma S. Sentiment analysis of public services for smart society: Literature review and future research directions. Government Information Quarterly. 2022;**39**(3):101708. DOI: 10.1016/j.giq.2022.101708 [Accessed: 1 July 2023]

[10] Alizadeh T, Sarkar S, Burgoyne S. Capturing citizen voice online: Enabling smart participatory local government. Cities. 2019;**95**:102400. DOI: 10.1016/j.cities.2019.102400 [Accessed: 1 July 2023]

[11] Hubert RB, Estevez E, Maguitman A, Janowski T. Analyzing and visualizing government-citizen interactions on twitter to support public policy-making, digital government. Research and Practice. 2020;**1**(2):15

[12] Alamoodi AH, Zaidan BB, Zaidan AA, Albahri OS, Mohammed KI, Malik RQ, et al. Expert Systems with Applications. 2021;**167**:114155

[13] Dini L, Bittar A. Emotion analysis on twitter: The hidden challenge, proceedings of the tenth international

conference on. Language Resources and Evaluation. 2016;**2016**:3953-3958

[14] Jabreel M, Moreno A. A deep learning-based approach for multi-label emotion classification in tweets. Applied Sciences. 2019;**9**(6):1123

[15] Mohammad SM, Bravo-Marquez F, Salame M, Kiritchenko S. Task 1: Affect in Tweets. In: Proceedings of The 12th International Workshop on Semantic Evaluation. New Orleans, LA, USA. 2018. pp. 1-17

[16] Dimitrov D, Baran E, Fafalios P, Yu R, Zhu X, Zloch M, et al. TweetsCOV19 – A knowledge base of semantically annotated tweets about the COVID19 pandemic. In: Proceedings of the 29th ACM International Conference on Information & Knowledge Management. (Online). 2020. pp. 2991-2998

[17] Lwin MO, Lu J, Sheldenkar A, Schulz PJ, Shin W, Gupta RK, et al. Global sentiments surrounding the COVID-19 pandemic on twitter: Analysis of twitter trends. JMIR Public Health and Surveillance. 2020;**6**(2):e19447

[18] Seki Y. Use of twitter for analysis of public sentiment for improvement of local government service. In: Proceeding of the 2nd IEEE Int'l Conf. On Smart Computing (SMARTCOMP 2016). St. Louis, MO, USA. 2016. pp. 325-327. DOI: 10.1109/SMARTCOMP. 2016.7501726 [Accessed: 1 July 2023]

[19] Martin JR, White PRR. The Language of Evaluation: Appraisal in English. London, UK: Palgrave Macmillan; 2005

[20] Caruana R. Multitask learning. Machine Learning. 1997;**28**(1):41-75. DOI: 10.1023/A:1007379606734 [Accessed: 1 July 2023]

[21] Devlin J, Chang MW, Lee K, Toutanova K. BERT: Pre-training of Deep Bidirectional Transformers for Language Understanding. In: Proceedings of the 2019 Conference of the North American Chapter of the Association for Computational Linguistics: Human Language Technologies. Vol. 1 (Long and Short Papers). Minneapolis, MN, USA. 2019. pp. 4171-4189

[22] Ishida T, Seki Y, Keyaki A, Kashino W, Kando N. Evaluation of citizen opinion extraction across cities (in Japanese). Journal of Natural Language Processing. 2022;**30**(2): 586-631. DOI: 10.5715/jnlp.30.586 [Accessed: 1 July 2023]

[23] Raffel C, Shazeer N, Roberts A, Lee K, Narang S, Michael M, et al. Exploring the limits of transfer learning with a unified text-to-text transformer, the. Journal of Machine Learning Research. 2020;**21**(101):5485-5551

[24] Putnam RD, Leonardi R, Nanetti R. Making DemocracyWork: Civic Traditions in Modern Italy. Princeton, NJ, JSA: Princeton University Press; 1994. p. 280

[25] Yonemaru S, Seki Y, Keyaki A, Kashino W, Kando N. Development of a Regional Social Connectivity Index Leveraging Twitter Data (in Japanese). In: Forum on Data Engineering and Information Management (DEIM 2023), Gifu, Japan. 2023, Article No. 5b-5-3

[26] Liu Y, Ott M, Goyal N, Du J, Joshi M, Chen D, et al. Roberta: A robustly optimized bert pretraining approach. arXiv:1907.11692. 2019

Chapter 6

Perspective Chapter: Embracing the Complexity of Human Emotion

Saeed Albarhami Thabit

Abstract

In this chapter, we delve into the multifaceted world of human emotions through the lens of advanced analysis techniques, aiming to unlock a deeper understanding of human behavior and decision-making processes in our digital landscape. We begin by illustrating the complexity of human emotions and the significance of accurate emotion detection across various applications, from marketing and customer relationship management to healthcare and social media monitoring. This context leads us to discuss state-of-the-art emotion detection methods, including transformer-based models, context-aware emotion detection, physiological signal recognition, and multimodal emotion analysis. Here, we adopt a systematic approach to emotion analysis, utilizing the transformer-based architecture fine-tuned on a tweets dataset. Our methodology achieves an accuracy of 82.53%, a precision of 82.79%, a recall of 82.53%, and an F1 score of 82.29% in predicting emotional categories. The chapter also scrutinizes challenges, limitations, and ethical considerations in this field, including ambiguity, subjectivity, and cross-cultural variations. Finally, we glance into the future of emotion analysis, focusing on integrating emotional intelligence into artificial intelligence systems and developing personalized techniques. We aim to spur further research and collaboration in this field, thus enriching our understanding of the dynamic role of human emotions in our interconnected world.

Keywords: emotion analysis, human emotions, emotional complexity, transformer-based models, multimodal emotion analysis, context-aware emotion detection, physiological signals, mental health monitoring, human behavior, decision-making processes, digital landscape, public opinion analysis, ethical considerations, cross-cultural variations, emotional intelligence, personalized emotion analysis, social media monitoring

1. Introduction

In our increasingly interconnected world, understanding the complexities of human emotions has become essential. In the digital landscape, the quest to understand and analyze complex human emotions has become more relevant through the lens of the most recent advanced emotion analysis techniques, setting the stage for a profound grasp of human behavior, communication, and decision-making processes. This chapter dives into the mysterious world of human emotions, employing advanced emotion analysis techniques as a powerful tool to unveil the underlying emotions that drive our actions and interactions.

We start by journeying into the labyrinth of human emotions, highlighting why understanding emotional complexity is crucial. The importance of accurate emotion analysis is discussed across various contexts, from marketing and customer relationship management, as emphasized in earlier research on the crucial role of polarity detection and emotion recognition in comprehending and forecasting customer service experiences [1, 2] to healthcare and social media monitoring, highlighted in past studies such as [2–6]. We then delve into cutting-edge techniques for complex emotion detection, including transformer-based models [7], multimodal emotion analysis [8, 9], context-aware emotion detection [10, 11]. We also discuss emotion recognition using physiological signals [4, 12–14] and address their potential to deepen our understanding of human emotions. The chapter also navigates emotion analysis's challenges, limitations, and ethical aspects, including issues like ambiguity, subjectivity, and cross-cultural variations in emotional expression, emphasizing a call to action for further research and collaboration to fully comprehend the multi-dimensional nature of human emotions in our digital era.

We conclude with a glimpse into the future of emotion analysis, accentuating the integration of emotional intelligence in AI systems, ethical considerations, and the emergence of personalized emotion analysis techniques tailored to individual preferences and cultural backgrounds. By offering a comprehensive view of recent advancements and challenges in emotion analysis, this chapter aims to inspire further research and collaboration, fostering a more profound understanding of the multi-dimensional nature of human emotions in our digital era.

2. Background

The landscape of human emotions is a rich tapestry woven with a multitude of feelings, emotions, and sentiments, varying in depth, complexity, and expression. Emotions are multifaceted and rarely exist in isolation, with humans often experiencing a blend of emotions simultaneously. Human nature's nuanced complexity offers intriguing possibilities and poses significant challenges for emotion analysis. Emotions are fundamentally subjective and deeply personal, making their accurate assessment challenging. To illustrate, consider the feeling of joy. One person's expression of joy could be another's expression of satisfaction, depending on their emotional and cultural background. This inherent subjectivity necessitates an intricate understanding of individual emotions in emotion analysis.

Emotions are also dynamic and ephemeral, changing rapidly in response to stimuli. The emotion behind words can change dramatically depending on the context or even the tone in which they are expressed. For instance, a person tweeting "I love this!" might convey genuine enthusiasm when discussing their favorite book but sarcasm when discussing a disliked policy. This demonstrates the necessity for emotion analysis models that consider the context and changes in emotion over time. Therefore, static emotion analysis models can often fall short, necessitating more dynamic and context-aware models that can adapt to the fluidity of human emotions.

Cultural and societal factors can profoundly influence emotional expression and interpretation. The same emotion can be expressed differently across cultures, and what might be perceived as a positive emotion in one culture could be seen as negative in another. Consider the example of a movie viewer watching a sad scene. One person might react with profound sadness, tears welling in their eyes, while another might feel a sense of nostalgic melancholy, yet another might be unmoved, deeming it overly sentimental. This variability in emotional reactions to the same stimulus underscores the personal nature of emotions, presenting a considerable challenge for emotion analysis. Consequently, understanding the cultural nuances of emotional expression and incorporating them into emotion analysis models is critical.

Furthermore, emotional complexity extends beyond verbal or textual expression. Non-verbal signals such as facial expressions and tone play an essential role in communicating emotions and are often more truthful than words. For example, when a person says "I am fine" with a neutral facial expression, their tone may reveal underlying sadness or frustration. This highlights the importance of multimodal emotion analysis, which integrates text, audio, and visual data to understand emotions comprehensively. Therefore, a comprehensive understanding of emotional complexity necessitates the incorporation of these non-verbal cues in emotion analysis.

The challenge of understanding emotional complexity underscores the significance of employing advanced emotion analysis techniques to navigate the complex emotional landscape, respect its intricacies, and accurately decode the underlying emotions. This challenging task of emotional understanding requires an amalgamation of linguistics, psychology, machine learning, and deep learning techniques. However, overcoming this challenge promises to revolutionize numerous fields, from marketing and customer relationship management to mental health monitoring and public opinion analysis.

Understanding emotional complexity is a vital prerequisite for the advancement of emotion analysis. By recognizing the multi-dimensional nature of human emotions and developing sophisticated techniques to capture these dimensions, we can better effectively and ethically harness the power of human emotions. This journey, as challenging as it is fascinating, provides immense opportunities for further research, collaboration, and innovation in emotion analysis.

As our understanding of emotional complexity deepens, numerous applications have started to benefit from this wealth of information. From personalized marketing to mental health support, emotion analysis allows us to tap into a human being's most intimate element – their emotions.

2.1 Personalized marketing and advertising

Personalized marketing and advertising have truly revolutionized traditional business practices, giving businesses a unique opportunity to engage with their audience more intimately. Emotion analysis, often conducted via advanced artificial intelligence technologies and emotion analysis tools, plays a pivotal role in this revolution, serving as the backbone for understanding and engaging with the complex emotional landscape of consumers. The heart of emotion analysis lies in the interpretation of the emotional states and reactions of customers. This process examines various customer feedback forms such as product reviews, social media commentary, or customer service interactions. By investigating these mediums, businesses can understand how their products or services are being emotionally received and perceived by the customers [2].

Emotion analysis can help reveal patterns of customer opinion that go unnoticed. For instance, it can bring to light a widespread emotion of disappointment in a product feature or unveil a sense of joy associated with a particular service experience.

This information can be further segmented by demographic groups, providing valuable insights into the emotional responses of different market segments.

Once these emotions are understood, businesses can adjust their marketing and advertising strategies accordingly. If the analysis reveals a negative emotion towards a product, the company may modify the marketing message to address and mitigate this negativity. On the other hand, if customers demonstrate a positive emotional response to a particular product feature or service, the company might amplify these emotions in their advertising campaigns, harnessing the power of positive affirmation to enhance customer loyalty and encourage repeat business.

Furthermore, emotion analysis can also be used to create more personalized and emotionally resonant marketing campaigns [10, 15, 16]. By understanding the specific emotions associated with a brand or product, companies can tailor their messaging to evoke similar emotions, creating a more profound and authentic connection with their audience. For example, a car company that finds its customers associate feelings of freedom and adventure with their products might develop advertising campaigns that evoke these emotions, resonating on a deeper, more personal level with their audience.

Emotion analysis in personalized marketing and advertising thus holds immense potential for fostering customer loyalty and engagement. As businesses refine their understanding of their customers' emotional responses, they will be better equipped to respond to their needs, tailor their products, and shape their messaging to resonate more deeply with their target audience. As such, emotion analysis represents a powerful tool in the modern business arsenal that promises to continue shaping the landscape of personalized marketing and advertising in the years to come.

2.2 Social media monitoring

Social media is a goldmine for emotion analysis. Social media platforms have precipitated a paradigm shift in how businesses interact with consumers and understand and monitor public opinion [3, 17]. Such platforms serve as a rich repository of public opinion, and when mined intelligently, they can provide unprecedented insights into consumer attitudes, needs, and behaviors. In this context, sentiment and emotion analysis applied to social media monitoring can be invaluable. For instance, consider a company's launch of a new product or service. By analyzing the social media discourse surrounding this launch—which could range from tweets to posts and photos to videos, a company can gain an in-depth understanding of public view towards the product or service. Moreover, sophisticated emotion analysis algorithms can uncover the polarity of the emotion (positive, negative, or neutral) and the nuances of the emotional responses elicited, such as excitement, disappointment, anticipation, confusion, or admiration.

Consider a tech company unveiling a new smartphone model as a hypothetical example. Emotion analysis of social media reactions could reveal that while the phone's design elicits positive emotions and excitement, its price generates disappointment or frustration. This nuanced understanding can inform the company's subsequent marketing strategies, pricing decisions, and design improvements for future models. The power of emotion analysis in social media monitoring extends beyond product launches. It can be employed to assess public reaction to advertising campaigns, gauge consumer satisfaction with customer service, monitor brand reputation, track emotion towards competitors, and identify emerging market trends or consumer needs.

By harnessing the power of sentiment and emotion analysis in social media monitoring, businesses can turn the tide of public opinion in their favor, make informed strategic decisions, and maintain a competitive edge in an increasingly digital marketplace.

2.3 Customer relationship management (CRM)

Within the domain of Customer Relationship Management (CRM), understanding emotional complexity allows businesses to respond to customer interactions promptly and empathetically. CRM has become a vital strategy in today's business landscape, where the customer is at the center of all operations. Using sentiment and emotion analysis within CRM frameworks is steering in a new era of personalized and emotionally aligned customer service, driving customer satisfaction and loyalty [1, 2].

A key aspect of CRM is interaction management, encompassing all touchpoints between a business and its customers. Here, emotion analysis can offer critical insights into a customer's mind. For instance, an email from a disgruntled customer might express disappointment or feeling undervalued. An advanced CRM system with emotion analysis capabilities can decipher these complex emotions, providing a nuanced understanding of the customer's feeling. This understanding empowers customer service representatives to respond empathetically and effectively, thus enhancing the overall customer experience. For instance, suppose a customer sends an email complaint about a recently purchased product that did not meet their expectations. A typical response might address the complaint at face value, offering a refund or replacement. However, with sentiment and emotion analysis, the CRM system could reveal underlying disappointment due to high expectations from the brand or annoyance at the inconvenience caused. Thus, the customer service representative could tailor their response to acknowledge these emotions, apologize, and offer a goodwill gesture, such as a discount on the next purchase. This tailored response will likely transform a potentially negative customer experience into a positive one, fostering customer loyalty.

In a broader sense, emotion analysis in CRM can aid in proactive issue resolution, trend identification, and strategic decision-making. For example, consistently high levels of frustration or disappointment related to a specific product or service aspect could prompt a business to investigate and rectify the underlying issue, potentially preventing a multitude of similar complaints in the future. By integrating emotion analysis into CRM systems, businesses can respond to customers more effectively and preempt issues, improve their offerings, and ultimately enhance customer satisfaction and loyalty.

2.4 Healthcare and mental health support

In healthcare, understanding patients' emotions can enhance patient-provider communication and potentially improve care delivery [2–5]. Healthcare providers can use emotion analysis to assess patients' feelings about their treatment, helping to adapt it better to suit their emotional needs. A patient's complex emotions might include fear, confusion, or hope, which could significantly impact their treatment and recovery process. Each application shows how embracing emotional complexity provides a richer understanding of human feeling, fostering more authentic and effective connections and solutions. By continuing to improve and develop emotion analysis techniques, we open up a world of possibilities for greater emotional understanding in our increasingly digital era. Prior research [18] demonstrated that social media can effectively detect and diagnose major depressive disorder through behavioral cues, while [19] highlighted the feasibility and efficacy of conversational agents like Woebot in delivering self-help interventions for anxiety and depression, emphasizing their potential as engaging tools for proactive mental health care. This empathetic interaction brings mental health support to those who might otherwise not have access, providing comfort and understanding in a non-judgmental, AI-powered space.

3. Literature review

In this literature review section, we explore the frontiers of emotion detection, examining the pioneering techniques that have emerged in this arena in the past few years. Advanced emotion analysis methodologies, analogous to precision instruments, can unravel the complex network of human emotions intricately, unveiling profound insights into our behavioral patterns, decision-making processes, and interpersonal dynamics. These sophisticated techniques not only cater to academic interest but are also designed in a manner that can captivate the curiosity of an everyday reader, owing to the universality of the emotional experience they decode.

3.1 Transformer-based models

The field of emotion analysis has undergone a profound transformation with the advent of transformer-based models such as BERT (Bidirectional Encoder Representations from Transformers) [20], GPT-3 (Generative Pretrained Transformer 3) [21], T5 (Text-to-Text Transfer Transformer) [22], and LLaMA (Large Language Model Meta AI) [23]. BERT employs bidirectional training of transformers, facilitating a nuanced understanding of word context by referencing the surrounding text. GPT-3, an autoregressive language model, utilizes machine learning techniques to generate human-like text. T5 innovatively reformulates every natural language processing task as a text-to-text problem, thereby training the model on diverse tasks. LLaMA, a collection of foundation language models, enables the adaptation of large pre-trained models to specific tasks, negating the necessity for extensive fine-tuning.

All these models, including their various adaptations, employ self-attention mechanisms [7]. This fundamental component of transformer architectures empowers models to assess the relevance of words in a sentence according to their contextual interrelation rather than their standalone significance. Consequently, this mechanism supports an understanding of the broader context of a sentence, including crucial linguistic elements such as negation.

Moreover, transformer-based models can also learn subtle emotional nuances crucial in complex emotion detection. Consider a statement such as, "It is a fine day." Here, the word "fine" may convey a cheerful or neutral emotion depending on the speaker's tone, context, and individual language usage habits. A model like BERT, pre-trained on a large text corpus, might have encountered similar usage patterns and could more accurately predict the intended emotion.

3.2 Context-aware emotion analysis

Context plays an important role in understanding human emotions. The same statement can hold different emotional connotations in different scenarios. Consider a tweet saying, "The final season was mind-blowing!" Without context, it is impossible to determine whether the emotion is positive (excitement about a television show season final) or negative (criticism of a political leader's final term). Context-aware emotion analysis approaches try to incorporate such context by considering additional information about the source, subject matter, or surrounding text or by using sophisticated models capable of learning contextual representations [10, 11].

Despite the advancement in LLMs (Large Language Models) that process vast amounts of text data using deep learning techniques to generate coherent and contextually relevant text resembling human language [24], such as transformer-based like "BERT, GPT-3, T5, LLaMA", and others [20–23] are designed to consider the context when processing text. The transformer architecture is built around self-attention [7], allowing the model to weigh the importance of each word in a sentence when trying to understand or generate a particular word. These models can take into account the broader context to a certain extent. Nevertheless, they only explicitly measure aspects like emotion or subjectivity if specifically trained to do so in tasks such as emotion analysis. However, their ability to account for context can benefit such tasks.

Context-aware emotion analysis is a more specialized task that explicitly seeks to understand the feeling in light of the broader context. So, in situations where understanding opinion is critical (like customer reviews and social media monitoring.), models specifically trained for context-aware emotion analysis could be more effective than a general-purpose transformer model. However, there is vastly active research in this area, and many of the latest transformer-based models are very good at tasks like emotion analysis, even in complex and nuanced situations. Nonetheless, they could be better, and there can still be instances where they might not fully capture the emotion, especially in cases where more profound domain knowledge or cultural understanding is required.

Consider the following hypothetical scenario: a sentence states," The company's latest yearly earnings report showed a decline in revenue but an increase in market share." Trying to find whether the sentence represents satisfaction and happiness or disappointment and fear can be difficult without context and domain knowledge, as it might be either positive(satisfaction) or negative(disappointment); for instance, considering the company in a highly competitive industry, "the company's latest yearly earnings report showed a decline in revenue but an increase in market share" might suggest that the company has successfully gained a larger market share than its competitors, indicating potential long-term growth and profitability, therefore, the overall message could be satisfaction and happiness. However, on the other hand, the company's latest yearly earnings report showed a decline in revenue might raise concerns about a negative trend in sales. Despite an increase in market share, the decline in revenue suggests challenges in attracting customers or generating sufficient sales, potentially impacting the company's overall financial health; therefore, the overall emotion could be disappointment and fear.

3.3 Emotion recognition using physiological signals

Recent advancements in wearable technology have opened up new avenues for emotion detection [9]. Wearable devices can capture physiological signals such as heart rate and skin temperature, galvanic skin response, and even brainwave patterns, which are demonstrably linked to emotional states. For example, a sudden spike in heart rate and skin temperature might indicate a state of excitement or stress. To illustrate, heart rate variability (HRV), the variation in time between each heartbeat, is a robust indicator of an individual's emotional state [9, 25]. Numerous studies have substantiated the correlation between HRV and emotions; for instance, an elevated heart rate and reduced HRV often signify a heightened emotional state, such as excitement or tension. Similarly, skin temperature is another physiological signal that varies with emotional changes. Research reveals that skin temperature increases during periods of intense emotional arousal due to the activation of the sympathetic nervous system. A sudden spike in skin temperature indicates a state of excitement, fear, or anger.

Moreover, Galvanic Skin Response (GSR), which measures changes in the skin's conductance, is highly sensitive to emotional arousal [16, 26]. An emotional event triggers the sweat glands, increasing skin conductance—a phenomenon that wearables can accurately measure, aiding in emotion recognition. Electroencephalogram (EEG) signals have also been used in emotion recognition, although more challenging to acquire outside clinical or research settings [16, 26, 27]. Brainwave patterns have been associated with different emotional states, opening up the possibility of emotion detection from EEG data.

However, it is important to note that these methods are relatively more invasive than emotion analysis based on text or speech, and their usage must comply with strict privacy and consent regulations. While these techniques are more intrusive and require user consent, analyzing physiological signals for emotion recognition has considerable potential for applications spanning various fields. These include but are not limited to health monitoring—where it can aid in diagnosing and treating mood disorders, stress management—by providing real-time biofeedback to users, and even the domain of personalized recommendations—where consumer emotional response to products can guide tailored marketing strategies.

3.4 Multimodal emotion analysis

While text is a critical channel for expressing emotions, it is not the sole medium through which emotions can be communicated or understood. Emotions are multidimensional and can be transmitted through a multitude of channels. Visual cues (like images or videos) and auditory signals (like tone or voice pitch) also carry crucial emotional information [28]. Multimodal emotion analysis incorporates these multiple data streams to derive a more holistic understanding of emotion.

Text-based models, including the most recent advanced transformer-based have indisputably revolutionized the field of emotion analysis concerning textual data. But, these models fall short in their capability to predict emotion expressed through visual or auditory mediums. In light of limitations identified by previous researchers [27, 29], which highlight the challenges of relying solely on text-based emotion analysis, implementing multimodal emotion analysis becomes critical. Multimodal emotion analysis, as detailed in [8, 9, 15, 30], is a method that offers a more precise and comprehensive overview of emotion by integrating insights from various data types such as text, audio, and video. For instance, during the evaluation of customer service calls, a customer might verbalize their satisfaction, yet underlying tones of frustration or disappointment might be discernable through their tone or hesitation. Likewise, in the analysis of video reviews, visual expressions prove essential in accurately conveying emotions, further underscoring the indispensable role of a multimodal approach in emotion analysis. Performing multimodal emotion analysis is a complex task that involves various steps and processes. The idea is to combine information from different modes (like text, audio, and video) to make predictions.

It is worth noting that aligning multimodal data can be a significant challenge, especially in scenarios where the data is collected independently or in an unstructured way. However, there are some strategies to ensure the correct association:

- Timestamps: If each data source (text, audio, video) has an associated timestamp, you could align the data based on these timestamps.

- Identifier Labels: If your data comes from a system that tags or labels each data entry with a unique identifier, you can use this to align your data.

- Sequential Alignment: If your data comes in a sequential or chronological order (for instance, a video transcript), you can correlate the data based on the order.

- Manual Alignment: Manual alignment can be performed if your dataset is not too large. This method can be very accurate but is time-consuming and requires many resources.

The aforementioned techniques are revolutionizing the way we understand and analyze human emotions. However, it is worth noting that each technique has strengths and weaknesses and may be more suited to particular applications than others. Furthermore, they all grapple with challenges such as ambiguity, subjectivity, and cultural variations in emotional expression, echoing the need for continuous research, refinement, and innovation in the field of emotion analysis.

Advanced emotion analysis techniques serve as our compass, guiding us towards a deeper and more nuanced understanding of our collective emotional landscape. Embracing emotional complexity is not an end goal but a continuous journey, like our understanding and exploration of human emotion.

4. Methodology

This analysis adopts a systematic approach to investigate human emotions within cloud providers' services. The methodology encompasses data collection, cleaning, preprocessing, exploratory data analysis, data splitting, model Fine-tuning, testing, and evaluation utilizing the transformer-based architecture as illustrated in (**Figure 1**). The following subsections provide a comprehensive outline of each phase:

4.1 Data collection

We rely on Twitter's Rest APIs as our primary data source to build a comprehensive and representative dataset, providing access to many tweets about cloud computing services. Twitter's large user base and concise tweet format make it an ideal platform for capturing and analyzing human emotions.

We have deliberately collected tweets as our primary data source to capture the nuanced and often ambiguous expression of human emotions. By avoiding pre-made datasets with predefined emotion labels, we aim to observe how our model performs in real-world scenarios where emotions are often conveyed in a complex and

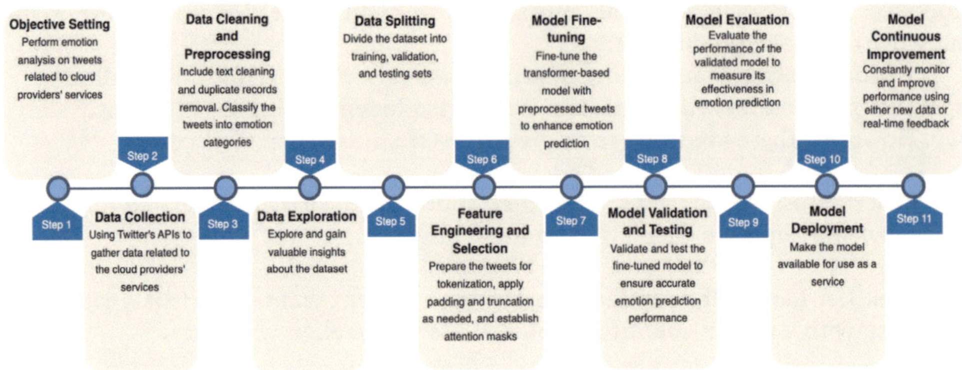

Figure 1.
Research methodology.

uncertain manner. This approach allows us to assess the model's ability to handle emotional expression's inherent variability and subtleties in social media contexts.

Our data collection strategy focuses on retrieving English language tweets utilizing specific hashtags such as "Azure, azurecloud, azure, AWS, awscloud, amazoncloud, GoogleCloud, GCPCloud, googlecloud". These hashtags are widely used in cloud computing discussions, ensuring the relevance of the collected data. We also exclude retweets to prioritize original content and capture authentic user emotion.

4.2 Data cleaning and preprocessing

The data cleaning and preprocessing phase in our research played a pivotal role in preparing our dataset of 9200 tweets for the subsequent stages of emotion analysis. We processed the raw tweets to remove extraneous elements such as URLs, user handles, hashtags, and certain punctuation marks. To minimize semantic discrepancies, we transformed the entire dataset into lowercase. Duplicate tweets were also identified and removed at this stage.

A crucial phase of our preprocessing involved identifying prospective emotion classes by applying the K-means clustering algorithm [31]. To ascertain the optimal number of clusters, we used the sum of squared errors across various cluster counts and capitalized on the elbow method, as shown in (**Figure 2**).

The count of clusters was further substantiated by visualizing the groups generated by the K-means algorithm and analyzing the inflection point on the plot of the Sum of Squared Errors (SSE) against the number of clusters, as depicted in (**Figure 3**). This visualization distinctly represented data points and cluster centers; each data point was color-coded according to its assigned group. Upon thoroughly assessing these visualizations, coupled with the outcomes of the elbow method, we determined that three represented the optimal number of clusters.

Through these comprehensive preprocessing steps and the utilization of unsupervised learning techniques, we gleaned valuable insights about potential emotion classes within our dataset, structured the raw data, and refined it into a form that optimizes the effectiveness and accuracy of our machine learning model. These actions formed the foundation for our subsequent manual labeling process and emotion prediction efforts. However, to get explicit emotion labels like 'anger' and 'joy,' we manually read through the tweets and assign emotions to the tweets dataset.

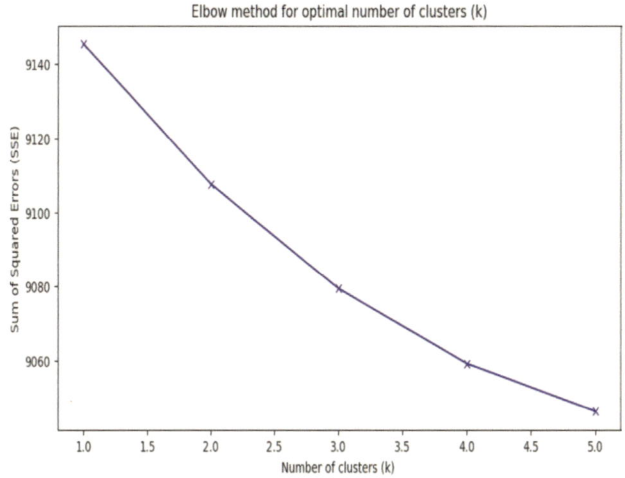

Figure 2.
Elbow analysis in K-means clustering.

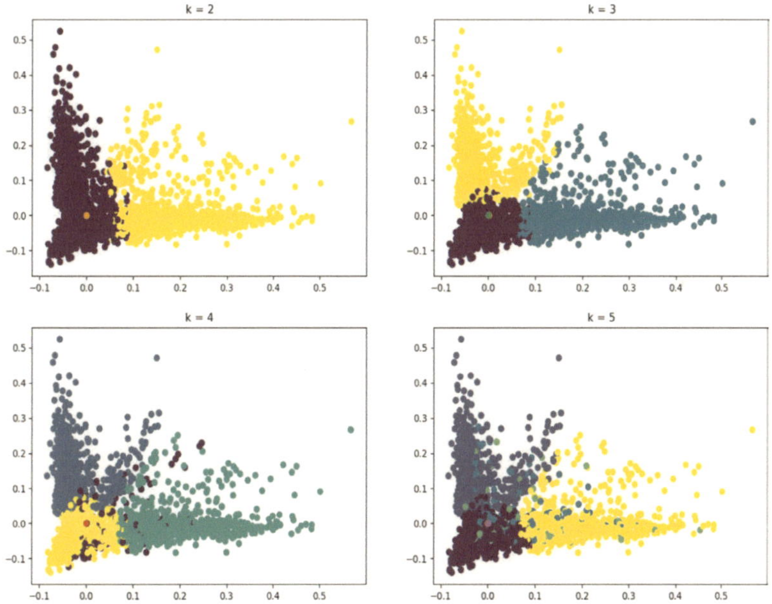

Figure 3.
Multiple K value in K-means clustering.

The data classification involved a harmonious blend of unsupervised learning and manual labeling. This mixed-methods approach allowed us to delineate complex emotion categories within our dataset and build a foundation for our emotion prediction model.

4.3 Data exploration

Exploratory Data Analysis plays a pivotal role in comprehending the dataset and discerning the inherent characteristics of tweets about cloud providers' services.

Total number of tweets	Average text length	Number of unique words
9200	108.073478	15958

Table 1.
Summary table.

Various visualization techniques were employed to explore the data effectively and gain valuable insights.

The following **Table 1** presents statistics, such as the total number of tweets, average text length, and the number of unique words, offering a concise overview of the dataset.

The word frequency, illustrated in (**Figure 4**), played a significant role in pinpointing common terms, offering key insights into the dominant linguistic patterns captured in the tweets. This depiction highlights the words that appear most frequently and contributes to a comprehensive understanding of the linguistic traits embodied within the dataset.

In parallel, the word cloud visualization (**Figure 5**) was instrumental in visually representing and illuminating prominent themes within the tweets dataset. The word cloud effectively highlighted the most significant terms by employing varying font sizes to denote word frequency or importance.

The subsequent **Table 2** summarizes the association between each tweet and its emotion. This provided an illustrative snapshot of the tweets dataset. This compilation, thus, forms a solid foundation for subsequent stages of our research, where these categories will be employed for further emotion analysis.

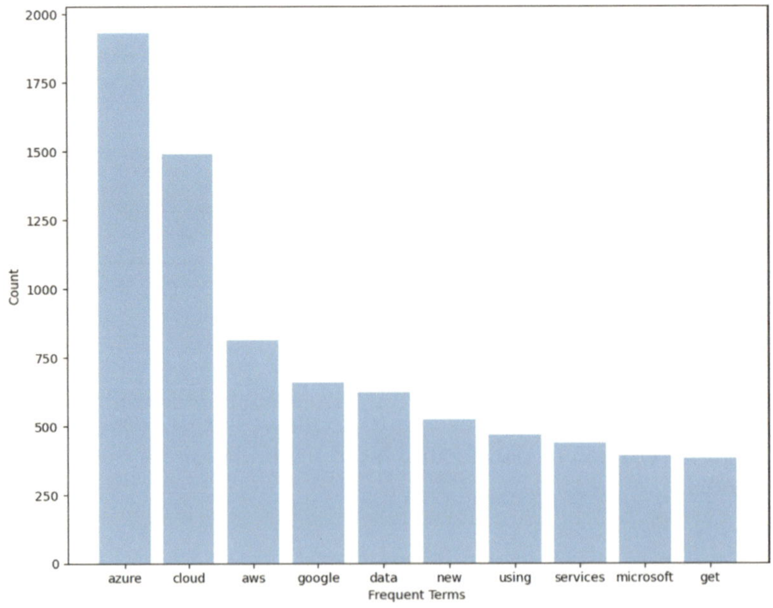

Figure 4.
Terms frequency.

Tweet	Emotion
If it was e.g. SharePoint we could simply add a script to the master page and everything would be covered. Why cannot we do something similar with PowerApps?	distress
Microsoft Azure DevOps server and team foundation server information disclosure vulnerability	distress
I love when we are professional in our explanations	joy
Function-as-a-Service? Demystifying serverless deployments with by Chris Kipp. Let us use Zeit Now platform as a super simple example of how easy it is to get applications up and running!	joy
Businesses use to obtain smarter and assure uninterrupted service delivery in environments. Find out how our for reduces risk and increases agility	neutral
Many games are already using Azure services for multiplayer games	neutral

Table 2.
Tweets with corresponding emotions.

Figure 5.
Prominent terms.

The bar chart, as portrayed in (**Figure 6**), was utilized to represent the diverse range of emotions in our dataset. Not only does this chart depict the distribution of each emotion, but it also shows their proportional representation relative to the entire data set. This allows for a clear visual comparison, highlighting the predominance or rarity of specific emotions.

The histogram, as visualized in (**Figure 7**), was systematically employed to uncover the underlying patterns and potential anomalies associated with the length of the tweets.

4.4 Data splitting

The cleaned dataset was split into training, validation, and test sets through stratified sampling, ensuring each set contained a representative proportion of samples for

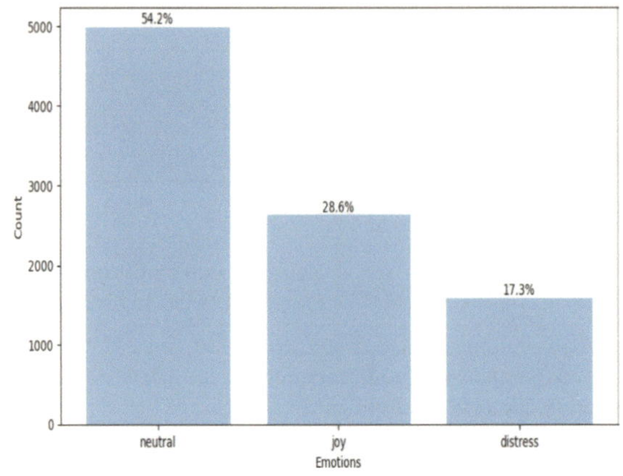

Figure 6.
Emotions distribution.

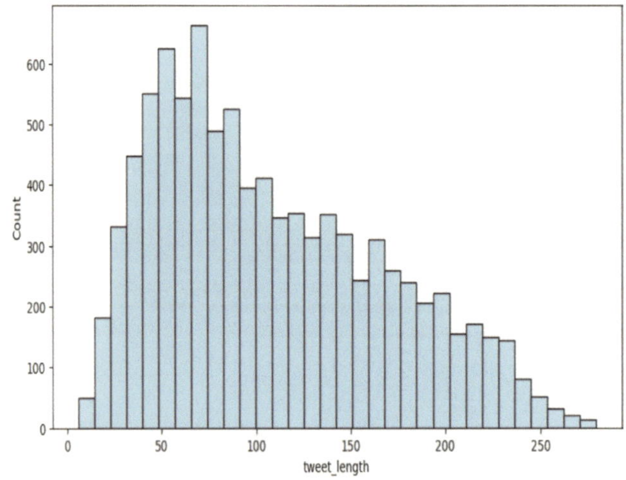

Figure 7.
The distribution of tweet text lengths.

each target emotion. This is an important consideration, especially for imbalanced datasets, ensuring that the balance of each emotion in the training, validation, and test sets mirrors that in the original dataset.

Following the data segregation, an analysis was conducted to understand the distribution of emotions across the different subsets. The distribution was visualized using a grouped bar chart (**Figure 8**), which exhibited the proportion of each emotion in the training, validation, and test datasets.

The following **Table 3** presents a summary of the emotion distribution in the tweets dataset. Each row represents a specific emotion, its corresponding encoding, and the count of tweets associated with that emotion. The dataset consists of 4982 tweets labeled as "neutral" (encoding: 2), 2628 tweets labeled as "joy" (encoding: 1), and 1590 tweets labeled as "distress" (encoding: 0). This information provides an overview of the distribution of emotions within the dataset and serves as a foundation for further analysis and modeling.

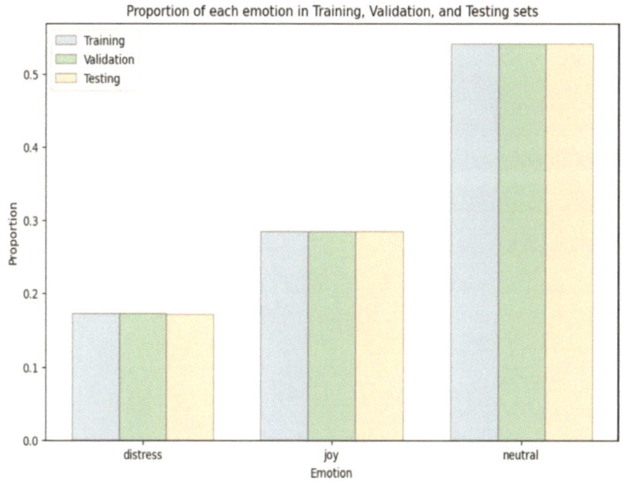

Figure 8.
Emotions distribution.

Label	Encoding	Count of tweets
Neutral	2	4982
Joy	1	2628
Distress	0	1590

Table 3.
Summary of emotion distribution in tweets.

4.5 Feature engineering and selection

In the feature engineering step within our methodology, the unprocessed tweet corpus was converted into a structured format compatible with the RoBERTa-based model. This process involved tokenization of the tweets into subwords, adjusting these sequences to a fixed length, and creating attention masks. Each component is critical in ensuring our model can accurately interpret the data.

The tokenization stage uses a pre-trained RoBERTa tokenizer to convert each tweet into a sequence of subword tokens. Each token is represented as a unique integer identifier. This approach mitigates the limitation of a fixed vocabulary and helps to preserve meaningful linguistic nuances that could otherwise be lost.

The below **Table 4** shows the properties of the token sequences and a statistical analysis of the lengths of these sequences post-tokenization. The summary statistics indicated that, from the corpus of 9200 tweets, the average token sequence length is approximately 24.48 tokens, with a standard deviation of 12.55. The shortest tokenized tweet consists of only three tokens, while the longest extends to 81 tokens. Notably, 50% of the tweets have a token length of 22 or fewer tokens, revealing a substantial skewness in the distribution towards shorter tweets.

Since transformer-based models require input data in uniform length, the sequences were padded or truncated to a pre-defined maximum length of 64 tokens. Padding is indispensable when the token length is less than the maximum defined

Statistic	Value
Count	9200
Mean	24.48
Standard deviation	12.55
Min	3
Median	22
Max	81

Table 4.
Statistics of token lengths.

length, filling the residual positions with a designated padding token. Conversely, for sequences exceeding the maximum size, truncation ensures the sequence is limited to the initial 64 tokens.

Upon achieving uniform token sequences, attention masks were generated for each tweet. An attention mask, essentially a binary tensor, indicates the positions containing actual content (denoted by 1 s) versus the padded positions (represented by 0 s). This plays a pivotal role in focusing the model's attention on the substantive content of each sequence, disregarding the irrelevant padded elements during self-attention computations.

To visually explain the distribution of content and padding across tweets, we created a heatmap as shown in (**Figure 9**) of the attention masks. In this heatmap, the x-axis signifies the token positions across a tweet, while the y-axis corresponds to individual tweets. Each cell's color intensity indicates whether the corresponding position is filled with content (darker shades) or padding (lighter shades). This visualization outlines the areas of real content in each tweet sequence, demonstrating the effectiveness of our feature engineering methodology.

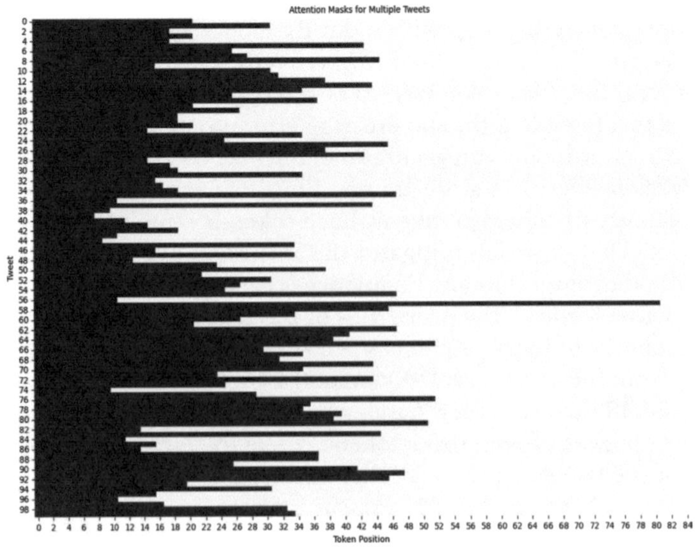

Figure 9.
Attention masks.

4.6 Model fine-tuning

The RoBERTa transformer-based architecture [32] was selected for its effectiveness in natural language processing tasks. The model was fine-tuned using the preprocessed dataset, optimizing its ability to accurately predict emotions associated with the tweets dataset regarding the cloud provider's services.

The model was trained over four epochs, concluding at 400 global steps with a final training loss of 0.47, as depicted in the following **Table 5**. Training loss consistently decreased, but an increase in validation loss after the fourth epoch signaled overfitting. The training process was halted after the fourth epoch to safeguard the model's capacity for generalization on unfamiliar data. Subsequently, the model was explicitly fine-tuned over these optimal four epochs. The research presents results from this optimal point, avoiding overfitting bias.

4.7 Model validation and testing

The model testing process involves testing the model using the test dataset. The model's predictions are obtained by performing inference on the test dataset, and these predictions are converted into class labels using a label mapping dictionary. The actual labels are also transformed into their corresponding emotion labels.

The following **Table 6** displays a subset of the predictions to summarize the model's performance. Each table row represents a tweet from the test dataset, with the "Tweet" column showing a truncated version of the tweet text. The "Token IDs" column represents a truncated version of the tokenized representation of the tweet.

Step	Training loss	Validation loss
100	0.911400	0.597774
200	0.522200	0.583825
300	0.444300	0.595613
400	0.346000	0.592506

Trained on a MacBook Pro with M2 Max processor (12-Core CPU, 38-Core GPU), and 32GB of unified memory. TrainOutput (global step = 400, training loss = 0.4781294107437134,total flos: 1125220975502400.0, epoch: 4.0).

Table 5.
Model training.

Tweet	Token IDs	Predicted	Actual
struggling with managing your cloud-comp ...	[0, 23543, 6149, 1527, 19], ...	distress	distress
certified with certifications yet? visi ...	[0, 25782, 3786, 19, 21045], ...	neutral	neutral
ready to transform your business with bi ...	[0, 16402, 7, 7891, 110], ...	joy	joy
enterprise customers are on the move to ...	[0, 11798, 22627, 916, 32], ...	neutral	neutral
wow! congratulations miles!! theyre l ...	[0, 34798, 27785, 24285, 1788], ...	joy	joy
hansis willhite earn academic all-distri ...	[0, 298, 1253, 354, 40], ...	joy	neutral

Table 6.
Tweet predictions.

The "Predicted" column displays the model's predicted emotion label for each tweet, while the "Actual" column indicates the ground truth emotion label for comparison.

The table serves as a means to compare the predicted and actual emotion labels for a subset of the test dataset, providing insights into the model's performance in accurately classifying emotions based on the input tweets. It offers valuable information regarding the model's ability to discern and predict emotions within the context.

4.8 Model evaluation

The performance of this model was evaluated using several widely accepted metrics, including accuracy, precision, recall, and the F1 score.

As depicted in the subsequent **Table 7**, the model achieved an accuracy of 82.53%. This indicates that, across all predictions, approximately 82.53% of the model's predictions matched the actual classes. This is a tangible result because our problem has more than two classes. Precision for our model stood at 82.79%. Precision measures how many of the model's positive predictions were correct. In other words, when our model predicted an emotion, it was correct about 82.79% of the time. The model's recall score was also 82.53%, matching the accuracy. Recall measures how well the model can find all the relevant cases within a dataset. The same recall and accuracy suggest a balanced distribution of class labels in the dataset, and the model is equally good at predicting all classes. The F1 score of the model, a harmonic mean of precision and recall, was 82.29%. The F1 score is a better metric when there are imbalanced classes, as it considers both false positives and false negatives.

The model showed varying performance in terms of per-class results as displayed in **Table 8**. The matrix illustrates the model's performance in predicting each class and the instances where it was incorrect. For the 'distress' class, the model accurately predicted 153 instances out of the actual distress samples. However, it incorrectly classified 3 instances as 'joy' and 83 instances as 'neutral.' In the case of the 'joy' class, the model demonstrated a relatively higher accuracy, correctly identifying 335 instances. Nevertheless, it misclassified 1 instance as 'distress' and 58 instances as 'neutral.' Regarding the 'neutral' class, the model achieved accurate predictions for 651 instances. However, it erroneously classified 21 instances as 'distress' and 75 instances as 'joy.'

Accuracy	Precision	Recall	F1 Score
0.8253623188405798	0.8279377007787103	0.8253623188405798	0.8229926445758601

Table 7.
Model evaluation metrics.

	Distress	Joy	Neutral
Distress	153	3	83
Joy	1	335	58
Neutral	21	75	651

Table 8.
Confusion matrix.

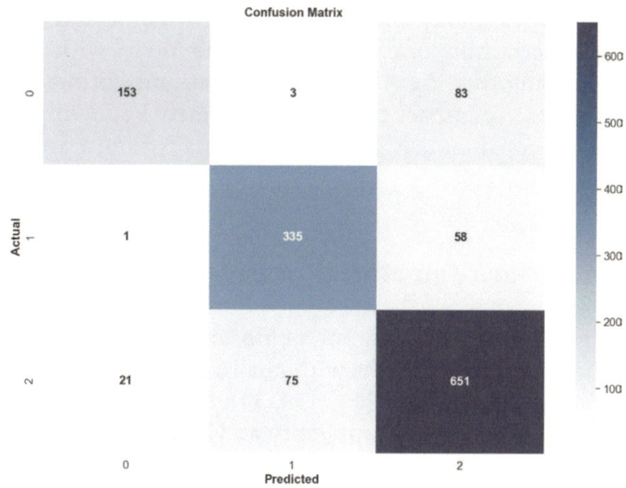

Figure 10.
Terms frequency bar chart.

The confusion matrix provides a comprehensive overview of the model's performance across different classes, revealing both correct predictions and misclassifications. This analysis offers valuable insights into the model's ability to distinguish between various emotional categories.

The confusion matrix (**Figure 10**) provides us with a perspective on model performance. Although the model has shown a reasonably good overall performance, it could be improved further, particularly in its ability to correctly predict 'distress' and 'neutral,' as indicated by the number of instances misclassified into these categories.

4.9 Model deployment

Model deployment refers to making a trained model available in a production environment, where it can provide predictions to new input data. In the context of our study, the deployment of the emotion analysis model involves wrapping the model into an Application Programming Interface (API), which can serve as a standardized interface for other software components to communicate with the model. Specifically, the API receives raw tweet data as input, preprocesses the data in the same way as during the model training phase, passes the preprocessed data to the model, and finally outputs the model's emotion predictions. The deployment of the model as an API offers several benefits. Firstly, it facilitates the integration of the model into existing systems or workflows, as these systems can interact with the model simply by making requests to the API. Secondly, it allows the model to be hosted on a server and concurrently provide predictions as a service to multiple users or systems.

4.10 Continuous improvement

For the continuous improvement of our model, we can leverage real-time feedback from users or fine-tune the model on new data. Users who disagree with the emotion prediction could submit the correct emotion, which can be stored alongside the original tweet. This valuable data can then be used for further fine-tuning our model. Furthermore, we should constantly monitor the model's performance in production, as the input data distribution may change over time, which could affect the model's performance. Regular retraining or fine-tuning of the model with recent data will be essential. Finally, ensuring that the API's performance and uptime are satisfactory is essential, as this can directly impact the user experience. Following these practices ensures that our model continuously improves and stays robust and valuable over time.

5. Challenges, limitations and ethical considerations

While the journey of deciphering human emotions through emotion analysis has proven fruitful, it has also been fraught with challenges and limitations [27, 29], encased in layers of ethical considerations [33, 34]. This section examines these aspects, highlighting their inherent complexity and the ongoing need for meticulous attention and innovation in addressing them.

5.1 Challenges

The primary challenge is human emotions' inherent ambiguity and subjectivity. Human language is replete with nuances, context-specific implications, and idiomatic expressions, making it challenging to assign a particular emotion accurately. For instance, sarcasm, an expressive form of emotion, often implies the opposite of the literal emotion, posing a significant challenge to emotion analysis algorithms. Another substantial challenge is dealing with the ever-evolving nature of language, especially in informal platforms like social media, where new slang and emoticons frequently appear. This dynamic environment necessitates continual learning and adaptation, pushing the boundaries of emotion analysis techniques.

5.2 Limitations

Despite rapid advancements, emotion analysis techniques are inherently limited in their ability to comprehend the full spectrum of human emotions due to their reliance on predefined categories and labels. While these techniques excel at identifying basic emotions such as joy, sadness, anger, and fear, they often falter when faced with more nuanced emotions such as sarcasm, irony, or mixed emotions. Moreover, most emotion analysis methods are primarily text-based, limiting their applicability in scenarios where emotions are conveyed through other means like tone, facial expressions, or body language. Even multimodal emotion analysis, which incorporates visual and auditory information, faces limitations due to the complexity and diversity of non-verbal emotional cues.

5.3 Ethical considerations

Emotion analysis, especially when applied at scale on social media and other digital platforms, raises several ethical questions. The first is the matter of privacy and consent. While public posts can be considered fair game, is it ethical to analyze a person's emotional state without explicit consent? Additionally, how the results of emotion analysis are used also poses ethical concerns. For example, using emotion analysis to manipulate public opinion, target vulnerable individuals, or perpetrate discrimination is ethically questionable. Furthermore, the risk of reinforcing biases presents another ethical dilemma. If an emotion analysis model is trained on biased data, it can perpetuate harmful stereotypes, leading to unfair outcomes. For instance, the model could falsely associate certain dialects or speech patterns with negative emotions, leading to discriminatory practices.

While emotion analysis offers powerful tools for understanding human emotions, it is not without its challenges, limitations, and ethical considerations. Ambiguity and subjectivity, evolving language norms, and the difficulty of capturing the full range of human emotions underscore the complexities involved. Ethical issues, including privacy, consent, and potential misuse of analysis results, further complicate matters. Therefore, continued research, careful methodological refinement, and thoughtful ethical guidelines are crucial to advancing emotion analysis in a manner that respects and upholds our shared human values.

6. Conclusion

In summary, this chapter has navigated through the nuanced universe of human feelings, employing cutting-edge emotion analysis methodologies. It underscores the layered nature of emotions and the crucial role of precise emotion detection spanning diverse applications. Forefront approaches, such as transformer-based models, multimodal emotion analysis that amalgamates text, audio, and visual data, context-aware emotion analysis that considers situational variables, and emotion recognition using physiological signals, have been under the spotlight with their contributions towards a comprehensive understanding of human emotions.

Our implementation of the transformer-based model on a tweets dataset achieved an accuracy of 82.53%, a precision of 82.79%, a recall of 82.53%, and an F1 score of 82.29%. These results underscore the efficacy of such models in understanding and predicting emotional categories. Their practical applications span sectors like personalized marketing, social media analytics, healthcare services, and customer relationship management, demonstrating the potential of emotion analysis to delve into the emotional dimensions of human behavior, facilitating more genuine connections and effective outcomes.

The discourse also highlights potential roadblocks, constraints, and ethical quandaries, such as interpretation difficulties, subjective bias, cultural diversities, and privacy-related issues. Further research should address these challenges, explore ways to reduce bias, and improve accuracy across diverse cultural contexts.

As we gaze into the future, emotion analysis will move towards a more integrated approach by incorporating emotional intelligence with artificial intelligence systems and tailoring techniques to individual needs. By weaving in emotional subtleties and accounting for cultural contexts, emotion analysis can offer a holistic insight into human emotions in our globally linked society. These advancements will be critical in grasping the complexity of emotions, which is pivotal for the progress of emotion analysis and the ethical and practical application of human emotions' power.

The expedition to decode the labyrinth of emotions fosters vast possibilities for more research, collaboration, and innovation. By tackling challenges, honing methodologies, and adhering to ethical norms, emotion analysis can sustain its evolution, paying heed to the complexities of human emotions while preserving our collective human values.

Author details

Saeed Albarhami Thabit
RIT, Dubai, UAE

*Address all correspondence to: sat5006@rit.edu

References

[1] Cambria E, Schuller B, Xia Y, Havasi C. New avenues in opinion mining and sentiment analysis. IEEE Intelligent Systems. 2013;**28**:15-21. ISSN 15411672. DOI: 10.1109/MIS.2013.30

[2] Bollen J, Mao H, Zeng X. Twitter mood predicts the stock market. Journal of Computational Science. 2011:1-8. ISSN 18777503;**2**. DOI: 10.1016/j.jocs.2010.12.007

[3] Liu B. Sentiment analysis and opinion mining. In: Synthesis Lectures on Human Language Technologies. Vol. 5. California, USA: Morgan & Claypool Publishers; 2012. ISSN 19474040. DOI: 10.2200/S00416ED1V01Y201204HLT016

[4] Shu L, Xie J, Yang M, Li Z, Li Z, Liao D, et al. A review of emotion recognition using physiological signals. Sensors. 2018;**18**:1-33. ISSN 14248220.

[5] Lovejoy CA, Buch V, Maruthappu M. Technology and mental health: The role of artificial intelligence. European Psychiatry. 2019;**55**:1-3. ISSN 17783585.

[6] Greaves F, Ramirez-Cano D, Millett C, Darzi A, Donaldson L. Harnessing the cloud of patient experience: Using social media to detect poor quality healthcare. BMJ Quality and Safety. 2013;**22**:183-186. ISSN 20445415.

[7] Vaswani A, Shazeer N, Parmar N, Uszkoreit J, Jones L, Gomez AN, et al. Attention is all you need. Advances in Neural Information Processing Systems. 2017;**2017**:1-9

[8] Soleymani M, Lichtenauer J, Pun T, Pantic M. A multimodal database for affect recognition and implicit tagging. IEEE Transactions on Affective Computing. 2012;**3**:42-55. ISSN 19493045. DOI: 10.1109/T-AFFC.2011.25

[9] Poria S, Chaturvedi I, Cambria E, Hussain A. Convolutional mkl based multimodal emotion recognition and sentiment analysis. Proceedings - IEEE International Conference on Data Mining, ICDM. 2017:439-448. DOI: 10.1109/ICDM.2016.178

[10] Hazarika D, Poria S, Zadeh A, Cambria E, Morency LP, Zimmermann R. Conversational memory network for emotion recognition in dyadic dialogue videos. Conference of the North American Chapter of the Association for Computational Linguistics: Human Language Technologies - Proceedings of the Conference. 2018;**1**:2122-2132. DOI: 10.18653/v1/n18-1193

[11] Zaheer M, Guruganesh G, Dubey A, Ainslie J, Alberti C, Ontanon S, et al. Big bird: Transformers for longer sequences. Advances in Neural Information Processing Systems. 2020;**2020**:93-110

[12] Yin Z, Zhao M, Wang Y, Yang J, Zhang J. Recognition of emotions using multimodal physiological signals and an ensemble deep learning model. Computer Methods and Programs in Biomedicine. 2017;**140**:93-110. ISSN 18727565. DOI: 10.1016/j.cmpb.2016.12.005

[13] Bota PJ, Wang C, Fred ALN, Da Silva HP. A review, current challenges, and future possibilities on emotion recognition using machine learning and physiological signals. IEEE Access. 2019;**7**:140990-141020. ISSN 21693536

[14] Chen J, Wang C, Wang K, Yin C, Zhao C, Tao X, et al. Heu emotion: A large-scale database for multimodal

emotion recognition in the wild. Neural Computing and Applications. 2021;**33**: 8669-8685. ISSN 14333058. DOI: 10.1007/s00521-020-05616-w

[15] Zadeh A, Chen M, Cambria E, Poria S, Morency LP. Tensor fusion network for multimodal sentiment analysis. In: Proceedings of the 2017 Conference on Empirical Methods in Natural Language Processing. Conference on Empirical Methods in Natural Language Processing. 2017;**2017**: 1103-1114. DOI: 10.18653/v1/d17-1115

[16] Subramanian R, Wache J, Abadi MK, Vieriu RL, Winkler S, Sebe N. Ascertain: Emotion and personality recognition using commercial sensors. IEEE Transactions on Affective Computing. 2018;**9**:147-160. ISSN 19493045. DOI: 10.1109/TAFFC.2016.2625250

[17] Karamitsos I, Albarhami S, Apostolopoulos C. Tweet sentiment analysis (tsa) for cloud providers using classification algorithms and latent semantic analysis. Journal of Data Analysis and Information Processing. 2019;**07**:276-294. ISSN 2327-7211. DOI: 10.4236/jdaip.2019.74016

[18] De Choudhury M, Gamon M, Counts S, Horvitz E. Predicting depression via social media. Proceedings of the 7th International Conference on Weblogs and Social Media. 2013;7:128-137. DOI: 10.1609/icwsm.v7i1.14432

[19] Fitzpatrick KK, Darcy A, Vierhile M. Delivering cognitive behavior therapy to young adults with symptoms of depression and anxiety using a fully automated conversational agent (woebot): A randomized controlled trial. JMIR Mental Health. 2017;**4**:1-9. ISSN 23687959. DOI: 10.2196/mental.7785

[20] Devlin J, Chang MW, Lee K, Toutanova K. Bert: Pre-training of deep bidirectional transformers for language understanding. Annual Conference of the North American Chapter of the Association for Computational Linguistics: Human Language Technologies (NAACL-HLT 2019). 2019;**1**:4171-4186

[21] Brown TB, Mann B, Ryder N, Subbiah M, Kaplan J, Dhariwal P, et al. Language models are few-shot learners. Advances in Neural Information Processing Systems. 2020;**2020**:1-19

[22] Raffel C, Shazeer N, Roberts A, Lee K, Narang S, Matena M, et al. Exploring the limits of transfer learning with a unified text-to-text transformer. Journal of Machine Learning Research. 2020;**21**:1-46. ISSN 15337928

[23] Touvron H, Lavril T, Izacard G, Martinet X, Lachaux MA, Lacroix T et al. Llama: Open and efficient foundation language models. arXiv. 2023:1-12. eprint - 2302.13971

[24] Radford A, Narasimhan K, Salimans T, Sutskever I, et al. Improving language understanding by generative pre-training. OpenAI. 2018:1-8

[25] Appelhans BM Luecken LJ. Heart rate variability as an index of regulated emotional responding. Review of General Psychology. 2006;**10**:229-240. ISSN 10892680

[26] Kwon YH, Shin SB, Kim SD. Electroencephalography based fusion two-dimensional (2d)-convolution neural networks (CNN) model for emotion recognition system. Sensors (Switzerland). 2018;**18**:1-12. ISSN 14248220. DOI: 10.3390/s18051383

[27] Zhang J, Yin Z, Chen P, Nichele S. Emotion recognition using multi-modal data and machine learning techniques: A

tutorial and review. Information Fusion. 2020;**59**:103-126. ISSN 15662535. DOI: 10.1016/j.inffus.2020.01.011

[28] Hubert Tsai YH, Bai S, Paul Pu Liang J, Kolter Z, Morency LP, Salakhutdinov R. Multimodal transformer for unaligned multimodal language sequences. In: Proceedings of the 57th Annual Meeting of the Association for Computational Linguistics. Association for Computational Linguistics. 2020:6558-6569. DOI: 10.18653/v1/p19-1656

[29] Poria S, Hazarika D, Majumder N, Mihalcea R. Beneath the tip of the iceberg: Current challenges and new directions in sentiment analysis research. IEEE Transactions on Affective Computing. 2023;**14**:108-132. ISSN 19493045. DOI: 10.1109/TAFFC.2020.3038167

[30] Zadeh A, Liang PP, Vanbriesen J, Poria S, Tong E, Cambria E, et al. Multimodal Language Analysis in the Wild: Cmu-Mosei Dataset and Interpretable Dynamic Fusion Graph. Vol. 1. Copenhagen, Denmark: Association for Computational Linguistics (ACL); 2018. ISBN 9781948087322. pp. 2236-2246. DOI: 10.18653/v1/p18-1208

[31] MacQueen J et al. Some methods for classification and analysis of multivariate observations. In: *Proceedings of the Fifth Berkeley Symposium on Mathematical Statistics and Probability*. Vol. 1. Oakland, CA, USA: University of California Press; 1967. pp. 281-297

[32] Liu Y, Ott M, Goyal N, Du J, Joshi M, Chen D et al. Roberta: A robustly optimized bert pretraining approach. Preprint Identifier: arXiv: 1907.11692. 2019:1-13

[33] Brent Daniel Mittelstadt and Luciano Floridi. The ethics of big data: Current and foreseeable issues in biomedical contexts. Science and Engineering Ethics. 2016;**22**:303-341. ISSN 14715546

[34] Datta A, Sen S, Zick Y. Algorithmic transparency via quantitative input influence: Theory and experiments with learning systems. Proceedings - 2016 IEEE Symposium on Security and Privacy. 2016;**2016**:598-617. DOI: 10.1109/SP.2016.42